Contents

Part 2 Expanding the firm

About this course

Whether you are at present at school or college, sooner or later you will be looking for a job. You will then want to know what happens to people in industry and commerce, and why they behave in the way they do.

Why do they seem always to be striking for higher wages?
Why are some people paid more than others?
Why can't many people get jobs at all?
Why are prices in the shops always rising?

It is these and similar questions that this course of study tries to answer.

However, because so many people are unemployed these days, you will be wondering about your chances of getting a job and, if you cannot, what you are going to do. Many people who are unable to get jobs or who lose their jobs through no fault of their own, try their hand at making a living by working for themselves. Some are very successful; others are not. When you leave school or college you may have to rely on the success of one of these small firms to provide you with a job, or you may eventually even decide to start up a small business of your own.

In order to help you understand better some of the problems of our industrial society, we shall start by imagining that we are going to set up our own small firm.

We shall decide to manufacture something – it might be something you have already made in craft lessons or it might be an entirely new idea. We shall then have to do some market research to see if people will buy it, how much they will pay for it and whether we can sell it at a profit.

We shall have to find out how to get the money to set up our factory and then study a real factory so that we shall know how to organise our own. We shall meet people doing all kinds of different jobs and no doubt we shall want to ask them about their jobs and what they think about them. We shall also have to find out the best ways of selling our product so we shall make a study of various shops and other ways in which goods are sold these days.

When we have made a success of our small firm we shall need to consider whether to expand. This will create a number of problems. Where should we build our new large factory? Should we get the extra money we need through the Stock Exchange? Will we require more expensive machinery? How shall we increase our orders? Again, we need to study a real factory but this time a large one, to find the answers to these questions.

For most of the time so far we have been thinking of ourselves as owners or managers, but now we ought to imagine ourselves as the workers in our firm. How can we organise ourselves so that we get a share of the increased profits? What kind of problems might come up in the firm, and how shall we deal with them? How can we get more pleasure out of our work?

Now that we have thought of ourselves as managers and as workers, it is time to put ourselves into the shoes of the consumers or customers. Do firms or shops try to deceive or even cheat us? What kind of protection do we need?

We have felt something of what it is like to be managers or employees or consumers. In real life we may be each of these at various times. Is there any conflict of interest between the different parts we as citizens shall play in our industrial society? For example, as a consumer I want firms to produce the kind of goods I need as cheaply as possible. But as an employee I want high wages and not to lose my job simply because people no longer require the goods my factory has always made. Can conflicts such as these be resolved?

Some goods and services are provided by private firms, others through local and national government. Have we got the balance right? How do local and national governments decide how much to spend and what to spend it on? Where do they get the money from? How do national governments try to stop such things as unemployment and rising prices? Should some people and some countries be far wealthier than others? Should the rich help to keep the poor? Could this be achieved fairly?

From these questions you can get some idea of the decisions which have to be made in this and every country. We shall try to understand how these decisions are made, and how we could influence them if we wished to do so.

We think you will find the work very interesting. Much of it will involve you in doing things, not just making notes and learning them. When your parents were at school, they were not able to do a course like this. Perhaps you might like to let them read this introduction. They may even wish to help you with some of the work. They will most likely enjoy it, too!

Part 1 Starting a small firm

Would you like to be your own boss? 1

When you have been looking at television you have probably watched scenes such as the following:

an argument between workers and their bosses about higher wages,

workers complaining about being made redundant,

a woman shopper complaining about rising prices and saying that manufacturers were getting too much profit,

someone complaining about industrial firms causing pollution by putting their waste products into a river.

During this course we are going to try to understand why people in business behave in the way they do.

When you leave school or college to go to work, you will almost certainly be employed by someone. You will be an employee – a worker – not an owner or a manager. You will soon find out how a worker feels and thinks, because you will be one yourself, but it will be very useful if you have some idea also why the boss behaves in the way he does. So this is where we will start.

About one and a half million people in Britain are their own bosses. They own or manage small firms – by 'small' we mean about one to fifty workers. Many of these owners started the firm themselves. Documents 1A and 1B give the case histories of two of these firms. Read them now.

As you see from these case histories, people usually start up in business in a trade they already know something about. They do so for the satisfaction of running things themselves, and often at first they work much harder for less money. Sometimes they never do as well as if they were working for someone else, but sometimes they do very well and expand and become big businesses. We shall be looking at expansion in the second part of our course.

There are three types of industries:

1 Primary industries which produce raw materials, e.g. mining iron ore, coal mining. Agriculture also is a major primary industry.

2 Secondary industries which manufacture products from raw materials. These products are sold as components to other manufacturers or direct to the consumer.

3 Tertiary industries or service industries. These do not manufacture a product but provide a service to industry or the consumer. Examples are shops, garages, hairdressers and banks.

Mining metal ores

Farming

Secondary industry

Making cloth

Tertiary industry

Garage

In an underdeveloped country most people are employed in primary industries. Often these countries depend mainly on one crop or mineral, e.g. in Africa, Ghana depends mainly on cocoa and Zaire mainly on copper. As countries develop, more and more people are employed in manufacturing, and in an industrially developed country, such as Britain, most people are employed in manufacturing and service industries. The proportion of people employed in service industries is gradually increasing.

To start up a business in a primary industry in a developed country such as Britain requires a lot of capital, and people who start up in business on their own usually start a small manufacturing firm or provide a service.

We are going to imagine ourselves setting up a small manufacturing enterprise. Discuss with your friends the kind of article you might manufacture. It must be fairly easy to make, and something which is sold direct to the customer (not, for example, an electric meter which is sold as a component to another manufacturer). Perhaps the work you have done in science or craft will give you some ideas. Like the people in Document 1A, you must have some reason why you think your product will sell.

If you were to invent some very novel device, you would want to prevent other people copying it. You can do this by registering it as a 'patent'. Make a list of all the articles you come across which have a patent number ('Pat. No.') stamped on them, or for which their inventors have applied for a patent ('Patent Pending' or 'Pat. Pend.').

Document 1A *'Bangles and Dangles' Ltd*

John, Jane and Paul went to a college of art and did a course in jewellery and silversmithing. John and Jane married in their last year at college. When they left college, John and Paul went to work for silversmiths and Jane worked in a jeweller's shop.

None of them really liked working for other people, because they felt that their abilities were not fully used – they were bored. They would like to have had the freedom to organise their own lives.

From their knowledge of the trade they felt that there was a need for a business to do small, quick repairs, to make up jewellery to customers' specifications and to produce good but relatively cheap hand-made jewellery for young people.

To get going they borrowed money from relations, arranged a £1000 overdraft from the bank and set up a small workshop in John and Jane's house. They sold their products on a stall in the market hall in the city where they lived.

They found they had to work very hard indeed, much harder than they had worked for someone else and at first they made less money.

However, they had been right in thinking that there was a big demand for good, cheap hand-made jewellery and they decided to pand.

In order to get more capital they formed a private limited company. They took a shop with a big workshop attached in the area of the city where many jewellers worked, but they also kept their stall in the market. They opened up similar stalls in neighbouring towns and they employed a representative to visit gift shops and persuade them to stock their wares.

They are now very prosperous and still expanding.

Document 1B *Green and Son, Carpenters*

Mr Green had worked all his life for a medium-sized firm of furniture makers. A lot of their work was school furniture, such as desks. When his son left school he went into the same firm.

At sixty Mr Green was very active, but he knew that at sixty-five he would have to retire. In his spare time he had done a lot of work for neighbours, putting up storm-porches and fitted cupboards, so he now decided to retire early from his old firm to form a full-time business with his son, partly so that he would be able to carry on working after sixty-five and partly so that his son would eventually have a business of his own.

However, soon after he started there was a bit of a slump and he was not able to get enough business. They were almost out of money altogether before trade picked up again and Mrs Green nearly had a nervous breakdown with worry.

In order to get more business they now erect wooden home-extensions also, but to do this they have to employ a brick-layer to build the foundations.

Business is still not good and sometimes the brick-layer employee takes home more than Mr Green the boss.

Will our product sell? 2

The first and probably the most difficult thing to decide is whether our product will sell, and if so at what rate it will sell (i.e. how many per week?) because this determines the size of factory we must set up.

In general, we wish to produce as much as possible to make as much profit as possible, but if we make a mistake and produce more than we can sell, we may go bankrupt.

One way of finding the answer to our question might be to make a prototype and ask people whether they would buy it and, if so, how much they would pay for it. What would be the difficulties in doing this?

We cannot ask all possible customers. We can afford the time to ask only a small sample, and the difficulty is to make sure that our small sample represents our customers as a whole. In 1936 an American magazine called *Literary Digest* took the largest sample ever known in order to discover who would win the presidential election in that year. The answer calculated from the replies proved in the event to be wrong. The reason was that the magazine sent questionnaires to a random selection of people chosen from telephone numbers and car registration numbers, and the people who own telephones and cars are not representative of the population as a whole. Furthermore, those who reply to questionnaires of this nature might not be a representative sample of those who were sent questionnaires.

We must therefore decide what factors will determine who would buy our product, and ensure that these are represented in our sample in the same proportions in which they exist in the population who will be asked to buy our product. Possible factors are sex, age, and income.

A statistician can calculate what size sample we must take in order to get the desired degree of certainty in our result. You may have done some work in sampling in mathematics; if not, try the following experiment.

There are four black jars labelled 1, 2, 3, and 4. Each contains red and yellow beads, and they are marked on the bottom (so that you cannot see the letter) as follows:

	Red	Yellow
A	10	40
B	20	30
C	30	20
D	40	10

Gently shake jar 1, extract a bead, and note its colour. Return the bead to the jar, shake gently, extract a second bead, note its colour. In this way extract five beads. Your record may be something like YRRYR. Do this sampling for each jar marked 1 to 4. From your experiment, can you tell with certainty which jar is A, which is B, etc.?

Repeat the experiment, this time taking a sample of ten (in ones) from each jar. Then try a sample of fifteen. How large must the sample be before you are certain which jar is which? What general conclusion can you draw from this experiment?

In general, market-research organisations cannot afford to take the size of the sample to give them the degree of certainty they would like.

Two methods of sampling which are widely used by market-research firms are as follows:

1   Three-stage random sampling

Within the area required, Parliamentary constituencies are chosen at random, and within each of the selected constituencies starting addresses are chosen at random from the electoral register. The interviewer calls at the starting address: if no-one is in, he calls at the next ascending house number, and so on until he makes an effective interview. After each effective call he misses out four dwellings before starting again. (Why do you think he does this?) If the interviewer comes to a turning, he turns into it and carries on as before (even if this is not now in ascending house numbers). (If this type of interviewing were done during the day-time, what kind of bias would there be in the result?)

2   Stratified random sample, or quota sample

The population can be divided into the occupational groupings shown in Table 2A.

TABLE 2A   Occupational Groupings

Group	Occupational type	Percentage of population
A	Higher managerial, administrative, or professional – e.g. company director, doctor, senior civil servant, headmaster	13%
B	Intermediate managerial, administrative, or professional – e.g. owner of medium-sized shop, industrial scientist, engineer, university lecturer	
C1	Junior managerial, administrative, or professional, plus supervisory and clerical – e.g. bank clerk, foreman, bus inspector	19%
C2	Skilled manual worker	32%
D	Semi-skilled and unskilled manual workers	36%
E	Those existing on state pensions without other income	

The interviewer is given a quota in which the numbers from each group are in the proportions shown in the table. He has to find the right number of people of each kind.

The advantage of this type of survey is that it may reveal that our product is particularly attractive to a particular section of the community. We can therefore slant our advertising at this group.

The second difficulty about market-survey work is framing questions. For example, a firm had invented a light-dimmer: this is a knob fitted instead of the light-switch so that you can control the brightness of the light. They wished to find out whether it would sell.

You might think they could send interviewers round the houses asking, 'Would you like to buy one of these?' 'How much would you pay for it?' People would be likely to say 'Yes' and to indicate that they would be prepared to pay quite a high price for it, but without really meaning it.

The firm did a stratified random sample of *men* using the questionnaire, Document 2A. What information would they have found out, and how would it be useful to them?

You are now to plan a market-research survey for your product. Write out a) instructions to the interviewer (based on three-stage random sampling or stratified random sampling), b) a questionnaire.

Market-research-type surveys are used not only to find out whether products would sell, but also by newspapers, for example, to sound out public opinion on various matters, such as which political party would win an election. From the work you have done you can see that the reliability of these must depend very much on how carefully the sampling is done and the way in which the questions are framed.

Sometimes institutions such as trade unions carry out referenda among their members, and again great care must be taken in framing the questions. For example, if a union received a pay offer which the national executive of the union were inclined to reject and go on strike for a better offer, they might ask:

1   'Do you wish to accept the present offer?'

2   'If not, are you willing to strike for a better offer?

     or 'Will you support your national executive in striking for a better offer?'

Why might the way in which the questions are framed get different answers?

Document 2A *Market-research survey on a 'dimmer' switch*

1 If a light-switch in your house gets broken, do you replace it yourself or get an electrician to do it?

2 If the answer to question 1 is 'self', ask, 'Are you yourself an electrician?'

3 If the answer to question 1 is 'get an electrician', ask, 'Have you had an electrician to work in your house recently?'

4 If the answer to question 3 is 'no', ask, 'If you needed an electrician, how would you find the name and address?'

5 Have you ever installed or had installed any special electrical fittings such as wall lighting or a fluorescent tube?

(Show the prototype dimmer and explain what it does.)

6 Which do you think is the most important reason why people might buy a 'dimmer'?:
  because they would like to have dim lights for relaxing and bright lights for working?
  because it would save electricity?

7 Can you think of any other reason why people might buy one?

8 In which rooms of the house do you think people might fit 'dimmers'?

9 If you saw these advertised in a newspaper or on TV and decided to buy one, would you fit it yourself or get an electrician to fit it?

10 How much would you expect to pay for one of these in a shop?

11 Comparing these with all the other things you would like to have, would you be likely to buy one of these
  a) in the near future?
  b) sometime?
  c) probably not at all?

Can we make a profit? 3

3.1 Deciding a price

From the results of our market research we shall be able to get some idea of the number of articles we might sell and the kind of price we might get. We must now calculate whether we can produce the articles so as to sell them at a profit.

In order to manufacture our product we shall:

a) buy or rent a factory and office,
b) buy or hire machinery,
c) pay wages to workers,
d) buy raw material or components.

Are there any other costs?

Some of these costs are the same whether the factory is producing only a few articles or working at full capacity. These are sometimes called *fixed costs*. Which are the fixed costs?

Some of the costs vary according to the number of articles produced. These are sometimes called the *variable costs*. Which are the variable costs?

Suppose the fixed costs are £50 000 per year and the variable costs are £100 per article. What would be the cost of each article if we produced 1000 articles per year?

What would be the cost of each article if we produced 2000 articles per year?

Why is the cost per article less if more are produced?

We must now decide what a reasonable profit would be. Suppose we must invest £100 000 to set up our business. If instead we invested this money in a building society, what interest would we get (before tax)? Why should we expect to get more if we invested the £100 000 in a business? What do you think would be a reasonable return on the £100 000?

One way of determining our price is to decide what number of articles we expect to produce each year, calculate the cost, add the total profit we expect, and divide by the number of articles. If the fixed costs are £50 000, the variable costs are £100 per article, we produce 1000 articles per year, and we hope for a total profit of £15 000, what price should we charge?

If we make 1500 articles per year and still charge the same price, what would the total profit be?

If we make only 500 articles per year, what would be the result?

Working on similar lines, carry out the following calculation: the fixed costs are £100 000 and the variable costs are £150 per article.

a) If we manufacture 2000 articles per year, at what price must we sell each article to produce a profit of £20 000 per year?

b) What would be the total profit if we made 3000 articles and sold them at the same price per article as in (a)?

c) What would be the result if we sold only 1000 articles at the same price per article as in (a)?

What we have been discussing is sometimes called 'cost-plus-profit' pricing. Research shows that a lot of goods are priced in this way. Of course the 'price' we have been discussing is the price at which the manufacturer sells to the retailer (usually a shopkeeper). The shopkeeper adds his own profit margin, and we shall discuss this in a later section.

If our product is similar to one which is already on the market, we can price it by comparison with our competitors. If they are charging considerably higher than the 'cost-plus-profit' price, we might fix our price just below theirs. Alternatively we might put our price the same or even a bit higher and hope that the customers assume from our advertising that our product has an important difference which makes it worth buying rather than our competitor's. We shall be thinking more about these kind of tactics later in the course.

Suppose the price we determine on a cost-plus-profit basis is considerably less than the price which market research shows that our customers would be willing to pay? Is it right to charge the higher price and make a very high profit?

3.2 'Break-even' point

Suppose that the fixed costs are £50000 per annum and the variable costs are £50 per article. Draw a graph, to an appropriate scale, of fixed costs against number of articles produced up to 1000 articles. On the same diagram draw the graph of total costs against number of articles produced.

Let us suppose we designed the factory to produce a maximum of 1000 articles per year. Let us assume that we might normally produce and sell 800. What is the total cost of the 800 articles?

We decide that a reasonable total profit is £12000. What would be the total selling price of 800 articles? Plot this as a point on your graph and draw a straight line from the origin through this point. What does this line tell you?

If sales fall below a certain number, you will make a loss not a profit. From your graph calculate the number of articles you must sell to break even, i.e. when the income from sales just equals the total costs.

Where does the money come from, and who gets the profits? 4

4.1 Getting money from a bank

We shall need to raise money for two main purposes:

a) To buy buildings and machinery. Money used in this way is usually called *fixed capital*.

b) To buy raw materials which we turn into finished products and sell to the consumer, thus earning money which is used to buy more raw materials. Money used in this way is called *circulating capital*.

The first thing which would probably occur to most of us is to go to a bank.

Document 4A describes an interview between someone who wishes to start a business and his bank manager. Study the document and then answer the following questions.

1   Why do you think that banks are often reluctant to make loans to new firms?

2   What is meant by collateral (e.g. for a bank loan)?

3   Why do banks need to charge interest on loans and overdrafts?

4   Mr B can have an overdraft of up to £1000 at 10% per annum. On 1 January he draws £500 and on 1 June another £500. On 31 August he repays £250, and on 31 December the other £750. Complete this schedule for his account:

Month	Amount outstanding	Monthly interest (10% per year)
January	£500	£4·17
February	£500	£4·17
March		
April		
May		
June	£1000	
July		
August		
September	£750	
October		
November		
December		

What is the total interest for the year? If he had had a bank loan of £1000 for a year at 10%, how much would he have paid in interest? Why can he not use only the cheaper of the two – loan and overdraft – to meet all his financial needs?

5 What other services can the bank provide to a small business?

6 What personal services do banks provide to individual customers?

4.2 Forming a limited company

When we set up in business there are several types of business organisation we might choose, each of which has its advantages and disadvantages. The characteristics of the different types of business unit are described in Document 4B. Use this information to answer the following questions:

1 Why might it be easier for a sole trader rather than a limited company to obtain credit from suppliers?

2 Why do you think it was necessary for a government at some time in the past to pass a Companies Act which allowed the formation of 'limited' companies?

3 Outline the procedure for the formation of a private limited company.

4 What protection does the founder of a private limited company have against being 'taken over'?

5 Suppose that, as a shareholder in a company, I object to the way in which the company is being directed. What can I do about it?

6 A company has issued 1000 £1 ordinary shares, of which I own 100. In one year the profit to be distributed is £500. What dividend shall I receive?

7 A small private limited company has the following capital structure:

10 000 12% preference shares of £1	£10 000
10 000 ordinary shares of £1	£10 000

Complete the table below:

Year	Trading profit £	Preference shares profit £	%	Ordinary shares profit £	%
1977	10 000	1200	12	8800	88
1978	5 000				
1979	2 000				
1980	1 000				

What conclusions can you draw about the relative advantages and disadvantages of owning preference or ordinary shares?

8 Why, if the business is successful, would holders of ordinary shares expect to get a greater return on their money than if they had invested it in a bank or a building society?

9 What else might the directors decide to do with part of the profits rather than distribute them to the shareholders?

10 Directors are expected to run a business to make as much money as possible for the shareholders (otherwise the shareholders might elect new directors at the next annual general meeting). In what ways might the interests of the shareholders clash with the interests of the workers?

11 What changes could be made in company law to ensure that directors run businesses in the interests of both shareholders and workers?

Document 4A *An interview with the bank manager*

A man who wishes to start a small business, Mr B, has arranged an interview with his bank manager, Mr M.

Mr B: In my letter I told you about my background and about the small business I would like to start. Can you lend me

"I sometimes wish that I, too, were working for myself, and not just for humanity."

(Reprinted with acknowledgement to Punch)

the money to get going?

Mr M : Well, first of all Mr B, what money are you putting into the firm yourself?

Mr B : All our savings, about £2000, and about £3000 I have borrowed from friends.

Mr M : Well, if instead of buying premises and machinery, you rent the buildings and hire machinery, you will not need a lot more money. We can lend it to you in two ways. One way is a bank loan. For example, we might lend you £1000 to be paid off over two years. The interest we would charge would be £200, so you would have to pay back £600 each year.

However, we should need some collateral – something which we could sell to get our money back if you went broke. For example, if you have already paid up over the £1000 we are lending on a life-assurance policy, we could use that.

Another way is by a bank overdraft – in other words, we let you overdraw on your current account. This will work out cheaper than a loan, but you can use the money only for circulating capital, not for fixed capital. We review overdrafts each year and, if national economic circumstances are tight, we sometimes have to press customers to reduce their overdrafts.

Bearing in mind that you have had a current account here for some time which you have never overdrawn, I am willing to offer you a loan of £500 if you can produce the collateral, and an overdraft of up to £500. Perhaps you would like time to consider it and let me know what you wish to do.

Document 4B *Chief types of business unit*

1 Sole proprietor

In this type of business, all the equity capital (capital for shares) is provided by one person. He or she gets all the profits, but they have unlimited liability, i.e. if the business loses money they may be made bankrupt and compelled to sell all their private property to pay their business debts. The British bankruptcy law is extremely exacting, and a bankrupt may be left with only the clothes he wears, his bedding, and the tools of his trade!

2 Partnership

In this type of business, the capital is provided by up to twenty people. Usually, although not necessarily, they draw up a legal agreement. Sometimes one or more of the partners provides capital but is not actively engaged in running the business, and such partners are often referred to as 'sleeping partners'. As with the sole proprietor, each of the partners has unlimited liability. Any partner may dissolve the partnership at any time he wishes.

3 The private limited company

The limited-liability or joint-stock company (which usually has the abbreviation 'Ltd' after the name in the case of a private company) has the following characteristics.

a) The minimum number of shareholders is two.

b) The shareholder's liability is limited to the nominal amount of his shareholding, which is usually the price paid for the shares when they were first issued. For example, if a person buys £1 shares when they are first issued, and pays the full £1 on each share, then he cannot be called upon to pay any more money if the firm becomes bankrupt. Some time later a second person might buy these shares from the first person for £0·50 each (paying less because the company has not been doing very well), but he is still not liable to pay out any more money at any future date because the full nominal value of the '£1 shares' was paid in the first place.

c) A private company cannot invite the public at large to buy its shares, and a shareholder cannot transfer shares to another person without the agreement of other shareholders.

d) In Britain, companies are formed in accordance with an Act of Parliament called the Companies Act. Since 1844 there have been a series of Companies Acts, the most recent being in 1976, 1980 and 1981. These lay down that a company is to be run by a board of directors and a company secretary, the minimum number of directors being one in the case of a private company. Directors are voted into office and are removable from office only by the shareholders at a general meeting; a general meeting must be held annually. The shareholders are not permitted to interfere with the directors' day-to-day management of the business, but the 1980 Companies Act permits a shareholder or shareholders to take the directors to court if they think that their interests are being, or are about to be, unfairly prejudiced. For example, if a managing director proposed to make a very large gift from company funds to a retiring director, a shareholder might take the managing director to court because it might mean less dividend for the shareholders.

When a company is formed, a solicitor draws up two documents: the 'memorandum of association' and the 'articles of association'. The memorandum of association is a statement of the rules by which the company will regulate its dealings with the outside world. The articles of association are concerned with the internal affairs

CERTIFICATE OF INCORPORATION

No. 889028

I hereby certify that

NO SUCH COMPANY LIMITED

is this day incorporated under the Companies Acts 1948 to 1981 and that the Company is limited.

Given under my hand at London the 15 February 1982

Assistant Registrar of Companies

SPECIMEN

C.173

of the company within the general framework of the memorandum of association. It sets out the company's regulations concerning such matters as the rights and voting powers of shareholders, the powers and duties of directors, and so on. All these arrangements must comply with the Companies Act.

When the memorandum and articles are sent to Companies House the Registrar of Companies issues a Certificate of Incorporation, and upon receipt of this a private company may commence trading.

e) All companies are required by the Companies Acts to supply certain information annually to the Department of Trade. They must give details of the shareholders, the directors, and the company's assets and mortgages etc., and they must file a copy of the accounts.

f) There are two main types of shares: preference shares and ordinary shares.

Preference shares have a fixed rate of interest which must be paid in full before any dividend is paid on the ordinary shares. Ordinary shares do not have a fixed rate of interest, but the holders divide between them the remainder of the profits after all other claims have been met.

Debentures are not really shares but loans. They have a fixed rate of interest, and this must be paid before there is any distribution of profits to either preference or ordinary shareholders. Debenture holders are not members of the company.

4　The public limited company

The main difference between a private limited company and a public limited company is that a private limited company cannot invite the public at large to buy its shares whereas a public limited company can do this (through the Stock Exchange). Thus a company which starts as private may wish to become public in order to raise more capital.

A public limited company (abbreviation PLC after the name) must have a minimum capital of £50 000. A private limited company which wishes to 'go public' must have an alteration made in its Memorandum of Association and it may then try to 'obtain a quotation' on the Stock Exchange (see Section 10).

How shall we organise our factory? 5

An interior view of a wire factory

5.1 A study of the Wyre Company Ltd

We now have the problem of how to organise our works. Document 5A is a study of a small firm of the size we might set up. Read it through carefully, and then answer the following questions.

1   How many staff were employed at the time of the study? Make up a diagram showing their relationship to each other within the works.

2   What advantages does this small firm have over larger firms within the same type of trade?

3   Why has this firm been able to expand?

4   What are the advantages and disadvantages to this firm of being located in an area which has other firms producing metal goods?

5   What are the advantages and disadvantages to the workers in a neighbourhood of having several firms employing similar kinds of workers?

6   Why do the employees apparently think it is not necessary under their particular circumstances to belong to a trade union?

7   As far as we can tell from this study, what appear to be the most important factors in making employees decide to stay with the firm?

5.2 A study of a local firm

You will have the opportunity to study a local firm but, before you go, use the following suggestions to make out a questionnaire.

1   List the products of the firm. How many of each article were produced last year?

2   How are the orders obtained?

3   Where does the raw material come from? Who orders it?

4   Who plans the production, and how do they do it?

5   What outside services does the firm use?

6   What office work is done? If you can, obtain samples of any forms used, and trace an order through from the time it is made to the time it is paid.

7   How is the factory located relative to other similar factories?

8   What is the trade-union membership? How is wage bargaining carried out?

9   What are the safety regulations for various jobs? How well are they observed?

10   What is the history of the firm?

11   What is the present capital structure and turnover?

12   Draw a diagram of the workshop, show how the work flows through it, and find out what job each person does.

13   Make out a questionnaire such as the following for each worker.

TYPE OF JOB............................. MALE/FEMALE
MARRIED/SINGLE

ASK: 'How important do you consider each of the following?'
Put a tick in one column against each.

	Very important	Fairly important	Not very important	Not at all important
a) High wages				
b) Working conditions				
c) Being able to talk while working				
d) Working with friends				
e) Interesting work				
f) Varied work				
g) Responsible work				
h) Canteen				
i) Social club				

ASK: 'Do you live near any of the people you work with?'
YES/NO

ASK: 'Do you see any of the people you work with outside work?'
OFTEN/NOT OFTEN

ASK: 'Is there any other job you would sooner do?'
> YES/NO
>> If yes, ask 'Why?' and 'Why don't you change to it?'

ASK: 'Do you expect any promotion?'

ASK: 'How did you receive your training for your present job?'

OBSERVE FOR YOURSELF:
Are they able to talk while working?   OFTEN/NOT OFTEN
Is the work interesting?   YES/NO
Is the work varied?   YES/NO
Is there any opportunity to plan their own work?   YES/NO
Is the work responsible?   YES/NO

When you have gathered all this information and written it up, try to answer the same questions that we asked in Section 5.1.

5.3 Planning our own factory

Having regard to what we have learnt from our studies, you are now to plan in detail a factory organisation to manufacture your own product.

You will obviously bear in mind efficiency of production, but you will probably have formed some ideas about the way in which workers like to have the job organised, and you may be able to incorporate some of these ideas into the planning of your factory.

Document 5A *The Wyre Company Limited*

(This document is based on a study of a Midlands firm, but certain details have been altered to prevent identification, and other details have been added to present a more general picture.)

History

In 1926 a Mr Wyre (now deceased) was employed by a Midlands firm. He made wire components for their main products. But as the trade depression developed there was no longer sufficient work to keep one man fully employed on this job, and he was made redundant. However, each of the firms in the area still required *some* wire work, so Mr Wyre set up a room in his house to produce the wire components for two or three firms.

Soon after, he took over a bicycle shop, and he and his son ran the shop and did the wirework in a back room of the shop.

When trade began to improve, Mr Wyre found that there were quite a lot of firms in the area who occasionally required a quantity of wire components for special jobs, and there were shops in the area who would sell articles such as wire wastepaper baskets, incinerators, and decorative wirework. Since Mr Wyre had a specialist knowledge of where to get different kinds of wire, the best wire for different jobs, and the techniques for handling it, he was in a good position to supply this trade.

He and six others (mostly family) put up money to form a private limited company, and he rented a small factory, employing about twelve people. The work gradually increased.

In 1955 the seven shareholders plus one other increased the share capital to £12000, so that they could move to a modern factory on a trading estate. In 1970 they employed about fifty people and the turnover was about £400000 per annum. The output is spread over a wide variety of products, but machinery guards and incinerators figure fairly prominently.

Organisation

The managing director and majority shareholder is Mr Wyre senior (son of the founder of the firm). His elder son is the sales director, who works with one representative. Their method is to look up in a trade directory such as Kelly's (most public libraries have a copy) the names of all the firms who might use wire products as components and the large shops who might require a run of their goods. They then visit these firms to see whether they have any requirements which Wyre Co. Ltd could produce more easily than their present supplier, or, in the case of a shop, they might persuade them to sell a line of goods which they had not hitherto carried. Most of their business now comes from previous customers or firms recommended to them by previous customers.

The sales director obtains a working drawing from the customer, or in some cases this is drawn up by the assistant works manager. The managing director works out a price and, if this is accepted, the works manager orders the wire and any other components which may be required, and organises the production run. Types of wire which are used frequently are kept in stock and replaced as used.

There are two types of production run (refer to figure 5A – plan of Wyre works).

Figure 5A. Plan of Wyre Works

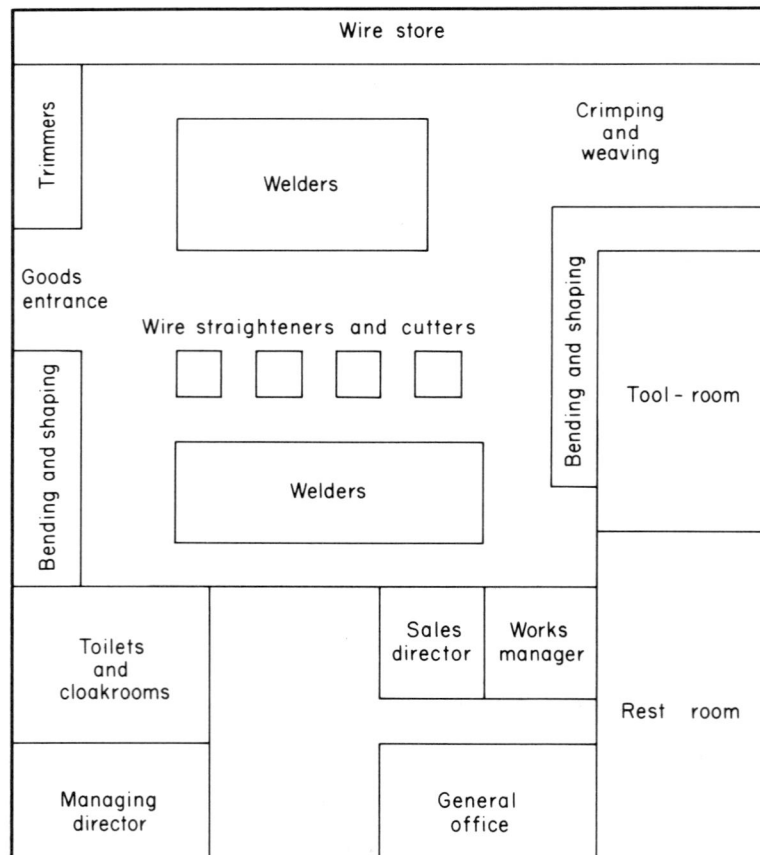

24

Straightening and cutting the wire

Trimming the components

Bending the wire

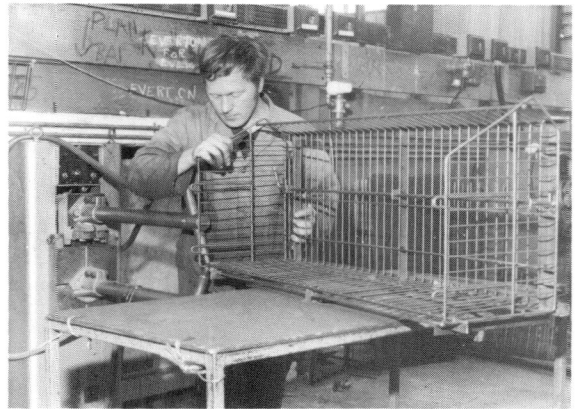
Attaching the wire to the sub-frames

Electric spot-welding

Plating the finished components

Most production runs start by the wire being straightened and cut into lengths. There are four electrically operated machines for doing this, attended by two men.

The wire then goes to the hand-operated bench presses for bending into shape. There are four

men and six women working in this section.
The components are then put together by electric spot welding. The jigs for doing this have been produced in the tool-room at the time the works manager planned the production run. About fifteen people (two men and thirteen women) work in the welding section, each working at their own individual machine.
The article then goes to the side benches again, for trimming. There are two men and three women working in this section.
The other type of production run is where the wire is crimped, then woven and attached to a metal frame. This is done by seven people operating hand presses and tools.
Occasionally some of the articles are hand painted, but mostly they are sent to other firms for electroplating or plastics coating. One man is employed as van driver.

The finished goods are sent by British Rail or British Road Services.

The making of the jigs and the care of the tools is done by one man in the tool-room.

The managing director's wife is company secretary, and there are two girls employed in the office on general clerical work.

The employees

None of the employees belong to a trade union, but the rates paid are the same as those in the larger union factories in the area.

There is no canteen, but there are facilities for heating up food. When the firm first moved to the new factory they had an hour for lunch, but the employees decided to reduce this to half an hour and leave earlier in the evening.

Most of the employees have been with the firm some time. The man in the tool-room has been with the firm the longest. Boys from school are encouraged to take apprenticeships and if they do they are given day-release, but they seldom decide to take them. It is difficult to get people to stay in the crimping-and-weaving section, and there is some turnover among the welders. Some of the welders move from one firm to another on the estate according to where the rates offered at a particular time are highest. The welders consider themselves more highly skilled than the side-bench workers. The side-bench workers have the most opportunity to talk to each other during working hours, and they have the most contact with each other outside working hours.

Selling our product 6

6.1 The retailer

Our problem is, what is the best way of distributing our product to the customer? But before we can answer this, we need to have some knowledge of the retail trade.

We can begin by looking at the way we buy goods in our own household. Take home the following questionnaire, and fill it in with the help of your parents. Fill in the answers to the best of your ability – if you don't know exactly how far away a particular shop is, estimate the distance as nearly as you can – but make sure you complete the questionnaire.

Type of Goods	How goods are bought						How far away?	How often used?	Average cost of item
	Inde-pendent shop	Multiple or variety chain store	Hyper-market	Dis-count store	Door to door	Mail order			
Groceries									
Greengroceries									
Meat									
Milk									
Bread									
Pharmaceuticals and cosmetics									
Sweets and tobacco									
Small household goods									
Clothes									
Shoes									
Furniture									
Electrical goods									
Newspapers									
Others:									

To help you, here is an explanation of each type of shop mentioned:

Independent shops

Small shops owned by independent shopkeeper, e.g. corner sweet shop. Sometimes they have joined together in voluntary chains such as Mace or Spar.

Multiple shops

Shops that have many branches around the country but which specialise in a particular type of goods. An example is Burton's for men's clothes.

Variety chain stores

Again, these shops have many branches around the country, but in each branch they sell a range of goods. An example is Littlewoods.

Hypermarkets

These are huge stores, covering perhaps hectares of ground, with parking space for hundreds of cars, situated outside towns and cities, usually with good access to motorways.

A multiple shop – the Burton shop in Southampton

Discount stores

Discount stores, such as Argos and Comet, may be thought of as supermarkets for consumer durables. (Consumer durables are items which last
a long time and therefore are not bought frequently, e.g. washing
machines, radios.)

Mail order

Here the shopper buys the goods using a catalogue, or an advertisement
in a newspaper or magazine, and the postal service. Examples of the
firms are Janet Frazer and Kays.

When you return the questionnaire, your teacher will help you summarise
the results for all your class.

1   Can you pick out any pattern from the information in the summary
    table?

2   Can you explain any pattern you pick out?

3   How might the pattern change if most families were to buy deep-
    freezes?

6.2 The wholesaler

Suppose you are the manager of a small hardware store. You sell a wide
variety of goods – tools, paints, wallpaper, etc. If in each case you traded
direct with the manufacturer, your time would be taken up by many visits
from the various manufacturers' representatives, and, since there are very
many small hardware shops, each manufacturer would need to employ a
large number of representatives.

It is in a situation such as this that a wholesaler can provide a valuable
service. He buys in bulk from each manufacturer and sells in smaller
quantities to the retailer. The situation can be represented diagrammatic-
ally, as shown on the next page.

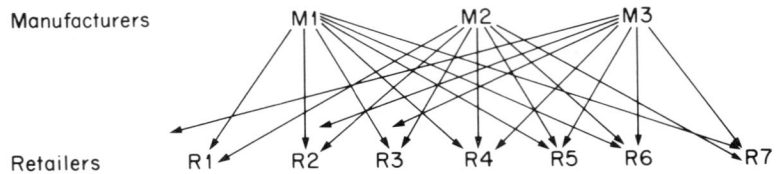

Manufacturers

M1   M2   M3

Retailers

R1 R2 R3 R4 R5 R6 R7

How many visits are required for each manufacturer to deal with each retailer?

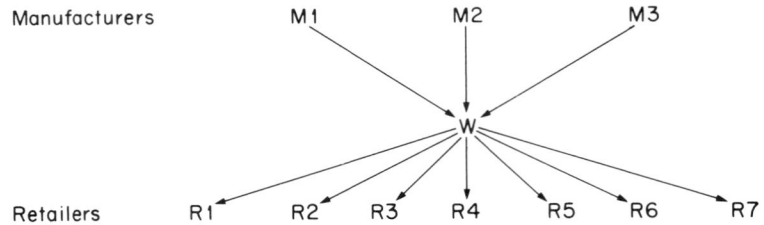

Manufacturers

M1   M2   M3

W

Retailers

R1 R2 R3 R4 R5 R6 R7

How many visits are required for each wholesaler to deal with each retailer?

Services which the wholesaler gives to the manufacturer and to the retailer

Services to the manufacturer:

1   He is able to inform manufacturers about the types of goods retailers are buying (and do not forget that retailers will want these goods as they are selling well in their shops). This can help the manufacturers to decide whether or not to increase the production of certain goods.

2   The manufacturer is able to devote his time and energy to *making* goods, as the wholesaler will buy them in large quantities and *store* them in his own warehouse.

3   The wholesaler will pay the manufacturer for the goods bought, promptly and in cash. The manufacturer is, therefore, able to use this to buy more raw materials, pay his labour, and produce more goods.

4   He transports goods to the retailers, thus freeing the manufacturer from this job.

5   He may pack the goods.

6   He is able to save the manufacturer a great deal of time, trouble, and money. Imagine a situation where a manufacturer had to deal directly with a large number of retail shops without the help of a wholesaler. The manufacturer would have to send bills, delivery notes, and all sorts of other communications to all the shops, and would have to hire extra staff to do all this. Postage costs would also increase, as would transport costs, for goods would have to be delivered in small quantities to many of these retailers.

The two diagrams should help to show the difference a wholesaler makes to the costs of a business.

Services to the retailer:

1   Retailers would find it very difficult and time-consuming if they had to deal with each manufacturer individually. The wholesaler offers goods from many manufacturers.

2   He sells to the retailer in small quantities.

3   He is generally situated near to the retailers and can supply the retailer quickly from his warehouse.

4   He is able to give the retailer advice on products, and can keep the retailer up to date with new products.

5   He is able to give credit to the retailer. This is very important to the small retail shops, as it is then possible to sell the goods to the public and then pay the wholesaler.

As can be seen, the wholesaler can be helpful to both the retailer and the manufacturer. Thus the traditional chain of distribution looks like this:

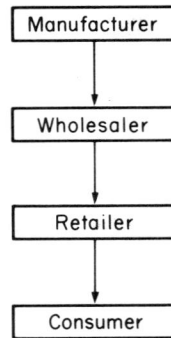

```
┌──────────────┐
│ Manufacturer │
└──────┬───────┘
       │
       ▼
┌──────────────┐
│  Wholesaler  │
└──────┬───────┘
       │
       ▼
┌──────────────┐
│   Retailer   │
└──────┬───────┘
       │
       ▼
┌──────────────┐
│   Consumer   │
└──────────────┘
```

1   To what extent would each of the following types of retail establishment use a wholesaler, if at all?
    a)   Independent shop selling a variety of low-cost goods – e.g. a grocer or a general hardware shop.
    b)   Independent shop selling high-cost goods – e.g. furniture.
    c)   Voluntary chain.
    d)   Multiple and variety chain shops.
    e)   Department store.
    f)   Mail order.

2   It is sometimes said that, if the wholesaler were omitted, the price of goods would fall as there would be no wholesaler's profit. Is this necessarily so?

3   Thinking of the product which you originally decided to manufacture, how would you decide to sell it?

6.3 Advantages and disadvantages of different methods of distribution
Now let us look in more detail at some of the types of selling units which comprise the retail trade.

1   Independent shops

There are a very large number of independent shops in this country. However, their total share of the retail trade is declining steadily, due to strong competition from other types of retail units, e.g. multiple shops and mail order.

The independent shop is generally situated conveniently for local customers – they are able to shop without going into town. The owner may also be more flexible with regard to his opening and closing times; for example, he may stay open until late in the evening and part of the day on Sunday. Regular customers might well be able to obtain credit and even a free delivery service. The shopkeeper may be prepared to exchange or alter goods with a minimum of fuss, and to cater for any special requirements of his customers. The atmosphere in the shop may be friendly and personal, with the shopkeeper often being willing and able to advise customers on the best articles for their requirements.

Prices, however, may be higher than in other larger stores, due to the fact that the small shopkeeper does not have the turnover or the storage space to buy his goods in large quantities and thus obtain discounts on bulk purchase from wholesalers or manufacturers. Due to his slow turnover, he may also find it difficult to keep up to date with new fashions and products, while being able to stock only a limited number of goods of any one variety. Due to lack of space, he might have to limit his display and advertising areas.

While the 'personal touch' in a small shop may appear inviting to the consumer, there is also the distinct possibility of delays in being served.

The small shopkeeper is often found in greater numbers in relatively low-rent areas, and this may help to keep prices down to a competitive level if the volume of trade is high. However, small shopkeepers must usually buy through several wholesalers, each of whom must meet his costs and make a profit.

2 Multiple and variety chain stores

These stores have been increasing their share of the retail trade. They are usually joint-stock companies who are able to raise greater amounts of money than the small shopkeeper. They buy in large quantities and pay promptly, and can, therefore, obtain substantial discounts from suppliers. They have very fast sales and can charge lower prices. In other words, they

A variety chain shop – in the centre of a modern shopping centre

can afford to make a smaller profit on each item sold because they sell so many. This means that total profits are still high.

These types of shops can also employ very skilled people who specialise in managing, buying, market research, etc. More use can also be made of such aids to selling as special offers, sales, etc. The buying of goods is done at the head office of the company, and the goods are then distributed to the shops. Although each shop has a manager, many of the important decisions are made by head office, for example, the buying of goods and advertising on a national scale. The manager, however, must be able to organise his stock, staff, and accounts. It may not be easy, however, to control a large number of branches without complicated and therefore costly administration.

These stores are generally found in the shopping centres and certain suburbs of towns and cities, where rents and rates are high. Their siting may not be as convenient to customers as the siting of independent shops. The goods that are sold tend to be highly standardised and do not necessarily cater for local or individual variations in taste and demand. Many of these shops rely on consumer self-service to a greater or lesser extent. Often a multiple shop may sell goods because of its reputation, and consumers will be attracted by its familiar name and shop front.

3   Department stores

Some large variety chain stores are organised in very distinct departments, and are often called department stores. These offer convenience to the customer in that many articles can be bought without moving from place to place. On the other hand, they are usually situated in the centre of large towns and so they may be inconvenient for the consumer who has to travel to them. The premises are large, with a number of floors. They are built on very expensive sites in the main shopping areas, where there are crowds. Sales floors are spacious, with plenty of room for the display of goods. Window displays are important, since an eye-catching display will bring goods to the notice of passers-by. Department stores provide a whole range of services to the customer, such as lounges, restaurants, hairdressers, escalators, lifts, pleasing decor, etc. They also provide experienced sales staff to advise customers on purchases.

For each kind of department e.g. the shoe department, a central buyer works at head office buying for all the stores in the chain in order to get discounts for bulk buying. However, in some stores the head of department has considerable freedom in ordering to meet local demand, and in some cases can do a certain amount of independent buying.

Payment for goods in a department store is generally made in cash or by a bank's credit card, but hire-purchase is often allowed on more expensive goods. Stores also operate monthly and/or budget accounts.

Many department stores now run mail-order departments to encourage customers who do not wish to travel. Because the shop is so large, other attractions can also be offered, e.g. exhibitions, demonstrations, Father Christmas, etc.

John Lewis – a department store in Oxford Street

An important feature of department stores is the seasonal sales, when the prices of many goods are cut to encourage customers to buy them. The store is able to clear much of its old stock by this method. Special cheap lines of goods may also be purchased by the store for resale during this period.

Other firms may be allowed to hire part of the store in order to sell their goods or services, e.g. Aquascutum and Susan Small.

Department stores have very high costs, e.g. rent, rates, wages, heating, lighting. These costs are often passed on to the consumer in the form of higher prices.

4   Supermarkets and self-service shopping

This has been one of the most important trends in retailing since the Second World War. Self-service as a method of selling is used now by many different types of shop, but one tends to associate this method with the multiple supermarket groups dealing with food. A self-service shop can only properly be called a supermarket if its area is at least 250 square metres.

Supermarkets deal mainly with goods that can be sold very rapidly; goods such as groceries and toilet requisites. They therefore buy in very large quantities and obtain handsome discounts. The goods are then sold to the consumer at the lowest price possible, thus increasing demand. Goods that have already been packed, wrapped, weighed, and priced are put on display for customers to see themselves. Once customers have made their selection, they pay for their purchases at the 'check-out points'.

A supermarket – large display shelves and trolleys for self-service

This method of selling reduces labour costs, since fewer sales staff are needed. In fact, staff are really necessary only to stock the shelves and collect the money for purchases, as service is cut to a minimum since there is generally neither credit nor delivery.

A great deal of time and effort is put into devising means by which the consumer is persuaded to buy the goods in the shop. Counters and shelves are carefully placed; the displays are eye-catching, with special offers and 'loss leaders'; and specially selected music may be played.

Many housewives regard supermarkets as a great help, as shopping can be done with the minimum of bother, although some prefer the independent shop because of the personal service and advice which is given. If the housewife wishes to buy only a few items, the independent shops may be more conveniently sited.

5   Hypermarkets

These are huge stores, covering perhaps several hectares of ground, with parking space for hundreds of cars, situated outside towns or cities. The stores sell both consumer durables and consumables on the supermarket principle. All the advantages of a supermarket are multiplied for the retailer, because of the huge turnover of goods, and all the usual supermarket sales techniques are applied.

This type of shopping is again only possible due to the wide ownership of motor cars. The hypermarket started, as did the supermarket, in America and has since spread to Europe, but the European country in which they have developed most is France, the biggest firm being Carrefour.

In Britain, Woolworth have established their Woolco hypermarkets, and several other firms such as Tesco have now entered this field.

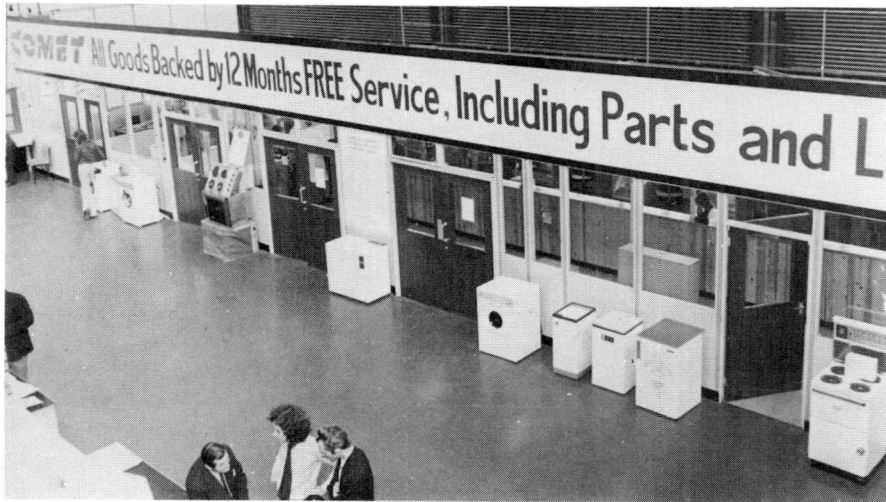

6 Discount stores

Discount stores, such as Argos and Comet, may be termed supermarkets for consumer durables. (Consumer durables are items which last a long time and which are not bought regularly – examples would be washing machines, television sets, and radios.)

The premises are often a large warehouse, which need not be sited in a high-rent area of a city centre since customers are prepared to travel a little distance (especially with the rise in car ownership) to buy these goods at a lower price – and this is precisely the reason for the rapid rise in popularity of these stores.

Service is cut to a minimum. The goods are stacked up with little pretence of display, and the customer buys what he wants and drives it away himself (discount stores generally charge if they have to deliver the goods).

7 Mail order

This type of selling method uses the postal service. There are mail-order firms who will send catalogues to prospective customers, and they may also employ agents to win custom for the firm. The agent is normally paid a 10% commission on any sales made. Credit is usually given on the goods bought. The catalogues contain a large variety of goods and are very expensive to produce. More than one is needed each year, the contents varying with the season.

Another type of mail-order firm advertises goods in newspapers and in magazines. Credit may still be offered. Postage and packing may be extra charges.

For the consumer, there is the convenience of being able to choose goods at home, and the credit facilities. However, the goods cannot be seen or

The cover of a mail order catalogue

touched before being ordered, and therefore quality cannot necessarily be assessed properly. There may also be delays in the post and further delays if the goods are faulty, broken, or of the wrong type. Exchanges or refunds of money may not always be granted readily, if at all.

Mail-order firms may be situated in low-rent areas and do not have to be close to large centres of population. There are no display or sales assistants' costs. The major cost may be the printing of the catalogue. However, there are costs – such as bad debts, postage, administration of the weekly credit payments, and the 'breaking down' of bulk – which all have to be met. These costs may mean that mail order is not necessarily a cheaper method of selling than a conventional shop, and therefore prices cannot automatically be expected to be any less.

Make a table like this:

	Manufacturer		Retailer		Consumer	
	Advantages	Disadvantages	Advantages	Disadvantages	Advantages	Disadvantages
Independent shop						
Multiple and variety stores						
Hypermarkets						
Discount stores						
Mail order						

Complete the table. Remember that what is an advantage to one might be a disadvantage to another.

Recent trends in retailing:

1   The Freezer store

A Bejam 'Freezer Food' Shop

An increasing number of households have bought deep freezers, and there are now shops which specialise in selling frozen foods in bulk, with a corresponding discount to the customer.

What do you think will be the effect on the pattern you observed in Section 6.1 if this trend continues?

2   Automatic vending machines

The principle is not new – cigarettes and chocolate have been sold by this method for many years. However, the range of these machines has grown recently, and such goods as petrol, beverages, and tights are now sold by this method. In some parts of the country, there are shops where various types of prepacked food are sold through automatic vending machines. America is again a leader in this field, and shops exist where the housewife can order her goods by using a punched card. The goods are then selected and packed automatically. These shops can, of course, be used by customers at any time, and the shoppers' time is saved. On the other hand, prices tend to be higher than usual, due to the cost of the complicated electronic equipment needed for this type of operation.

Vending machines selling fresh drinks

6.4 A study of a large store

1   Read through Document 6A. What would be the important differences in your way of life if you worked in a shop rather than in a factory or an office? Which of the jobs described would you most like to do? Are there any aspects of the job you would not like?

2   Imagine you are a sales assistant. Which of the following do you think

is the most important? Number them from 1 to 6 in order of importance:

being clean and tidily dressed,

keeping your part of the shop clean and tidy,

leaving other jobs in order to wait on a customer immediately she requires your attention,

giving the customer accurate information about the goods on sale,

making the customer feel that she has enjoyed being in your shop,

doing exactly what the departmental sales manager tells you to do.

3 From your own experience as a customer, which of the above do you feel that sales assistants consider to be the *least* important?

4 For each of the following statements, say whether you think it is true of all customers, true of some, partly true of all, partly true of some, or not true at all:

The customer knows exactly what she wants and she comes into the shop just to buy it.

The customer knows vaguely what she wants, but she needs some help in making a choice.

Most customers go shopping to give themselves a treat by buying something.

Many customers go shopping because they are lonely or bored and want something to do.

5 All the goods on sale in this store could be plastic-wrapped and sold in a supermarket-style store: the goods could be sold cheaper because fewer assistants need be employed. Why do many customers prefer to trade in a department store of this type?

6 'The customer is always right.' Say why you agree or disagree.

7 Plan the layout of a shop with the departments listed in Document 6A. Bear in mind that you want the customer to buy as many things as possible. Which articles are they most likely to come into the shop on purpose to buy? Which articles are they most likely to buy on impulse? You may decide to design the shop so that the customer must pass through 'impulse' departments on the way to and from the departments she intends to get to. Remember that children are accompanied by mothers.

Write a short account explaining your design.

8 Are there any goods you would add to the range sold in this shop?

9 At what times during the year might you expect trade to be slackest? What device do shops use to improve trade at these times?

10 The management decided to pay a commission on sales to the assistants. Do you think this is a good idea? Which would be the fairest: to pay according to the sales by individual assistants, according to the sales by departments, or according to the sales by the store as a whole?

Document 6A *A study of a large store*

This store is situated in the main shopping centre of a town of 40 000 people. It is part of a chain of similar shops.

There are twelve selling departments, each under a departmental sales manager (who used to be called a buyer). The departments are as follows (number of assistants in brackets):

coats and suits (3),
gowns (3),
millinery (2),
blouses and knitwear (3),
teenage fashions (2),
childrens (2),
underwear (4),
dress fabrics (3),
haberdashery and knitting wools (5),
handbags, luggage, and fancy goods (3),
gloves, hosiery, and perfumery (10).

In this latter department, three of the assistants are employed by hosiery firms (Wolsey, Pretty Polly, and Charnos) to sell their own particular brand, and five of the assistants are paid partly by the firm and partly by a particular cosmetic manufacturer (Elizabeth Arden, Charles of the Ritz, etc.).

Most of the goods are bought by 'head office' and distributed to the shop. The departmental sales managers are responsible for recording deliveries and sales, ordering replacement stock, and requesting items from the firm's catalogue which they think will sell well. They also have control over a certain amount of money with which to order special lines from manufacturers: they must use their own judgment to order what they think will sell well in their department. (In some department stores all goods are bought centrally, whereas in others the departmental sales managers or buyers are responsible for all their own ordering. This firm operates a mixed system.)

In addition to the selling departments there are the display department (a manager and two assistants responsible for window dressing), dispatch (responsible for accepting deliveries and distributing to departments, and dispatching goods to customers), maintenance, and office (four staff responsible for accounts and wages).

All the departmental managers are responsible to the general manager of the store.

Most of the staff are women. School-leavers or married women without previous experience are given a short induction course (about eight hours) in which they are taught how to deal with the various ways of making a purchase (cash, cheque, credit), how to operate the till, and how to parcel up purchases. Their departmental sales manager teaches them how to behave towards customers.

All those who are interested are encouraged to train as departmental sales managers. This training can be started any time after the age of eighteen, and it lasts for two years. It involves working in various departments, and part-time study in the business-studies department at the local college of further education.

Senior management (general managers of stores and head-office buying staff) are recruited from specially selected departmental sales managers or university graduates. They are given a two-year training in the larger stores of the company, with some time at a business college and at head office. After that they become assistant general manager of one of the large stores or general manager of one of the smaller stores.

Document 6B *Combines in the retail trade*

Cooperative Movement
Shops, stores and supermarkets organised in over 200 local retail societies.
Over 100 000 employees.
Supply food, clothing, shoes, furnishing, coal, etc.
Many own brand goods manufactured and supplied by the Cooperative Wholesale Society which has over 25 000 employees.

Associated British Foods
Controls a large and diverse food manufacturing and retailing empire.
Includes Allied Mills (flour mills), Allied Bakeries, Sunblest Bakeries, Fine Fare.
Subsidiaries in Eire, Australia and South Africa.
Over 71 000 employees.

Tesco
About 800 supermarkets and stores; over 35 000 employees.

Sainsbury
Mainly groceries. Over 200 branches and over 30 000 employees.

Great Universal Stores
Over 2500 shops and warehouses; over 35 000 employees.
Includes:
  Mens clothing: Hector Powe, Hope Brothers, Willerby.
  Furnishings: Cavendish, Times, Waring and Gillow.
  Mail Order: G.U.S., Kay's (the largest mail order business in Europe).
Also owns extensive factories and warehouses

Marks and Spencers
Branches in most towns; about 40 000 employees.

United Drapery Stores
Over 1000 stores and shops and 25 000 employees.
Includes John Collier, Alexandre, Richard Shops, Swears and Wells, Timpson, Stead and Simpson.

House of Fraser
Over 100 stores and shops and 25 000 employees.
Includes Harrods, Rackhams, Army and Navy.

Debenhams
Over 200 stores and shops and 30 000 employees.
Includes Hardy Amies, Lotus Shoes, Marshall and Snelgrove.

John Lewis Partnership
Over 60 stores and shops and 20 000 employees.
Includes Waitrose supermarkets.

British Shoe Corporation
About 2000 shops and 45 000 employees.
Includes Lilley and Skinner, Dolcis, Saxone, True-Form, Freeman Hardy and Willis.

The Burton Group
Over 800 retail outlets and about 20 000 employees.
Controls Ryman's, Jackson's, Peter Robinson, Evans (Outsizes).

Woolworth
Shops in most towns. Over 40 000 employees.

The Boots Co.
Shops in most towns.
Controls also Crookes Laboratories and Timothy Whites shops. Subsidiaries in many countries.
Over 60 000 employees.

Managing a small firm 7

In this first part of our course we have imagined that we have set up a small firm. You may have got the idea that all you have to do is to set up a firm and then stand back while the money rolls in! In practice, however, the manager of a small firm has many problems, and it is all too easy to go bankrupt – sometimes just when you think business is doing well.

We are going to play a game which will help you to appreciate some of the manager's problems.

Suppose that you have set up a private limited company, with a fully paid-up ordinary-share capital of £4000. You have hired a plant capable of producing up to 100 articles per quarter. The fixed costs are £1000 per quarter and the variable costs are £20 per article. Your market research tells you that initially you can expect to sell about 60 articles per quarter, but the number may be higher if you fix a low price and lower if you fix a high price. The number of sales may change both up and down as time goes on.

You will be given copies of the 'Quarterly Decision Form' (see example over the page).

1   Decide on your output and fill in item 1 under 'Production and sales' (maximum output 100).

2   Fill in the 'Costs' column in order to calculate the cost of each item.

3   Decide on a price.

4   Show your decision form to the teacher, who will fill in the sales (item 4 under 'Production and sales'). Remember, the lower the price the higher the sales, and vice versa.

5   Fill in the 'Revenue' column. In period 1, starting cash is £4000. (How can you work out whether you have made a profit in this period?)

6   Complete item 5 in the 'Production and sales' column.

7   Turn to the next 'Quarterly Decision Form'.
   a) Fill in the stock brought forward (item 2), which is the unsold goods (item 5) from the previous form.
   b) Fill in 'Starting cash', which is the 'Cash in hand' from the previous form.

8   Carry on as from number 1 above.

You will continue to play this game for a number of 'years', and the aim is to make as much profit as possible.

Quarterly Decision Form

Company.................... Year .... Quarter ....

Price ....

COSTS	£	REVENUE	£
Total Fixed Costs	1000	Starting cash	
Total Variable Costs (£20 per article)	————	Income from sales (price × sales)	————
TOTAL COSTS	═══	TOTAL INCOME	
Average costs, i.e.		Less costs	————
$\dfrac{\text{Total Costs}}{\text{Output}} =$	————	CASH IN HAND (becomes starting cash on the next decision form)	————

Production and Sales

(1) Output this period
   (determines total
   variable costs)

(2) Stock brought forward
   (output not sold last
   quarter) ————————

(3) TOTAL GOODS FOR SALE ———————— (1+2)

(4) Sales this quarter
   (depends on price charged
   and found out from teacher) ————————

(5) Unsold goods
   (becomes stock brought
   forward on next decision   (3−4)
   sheet)
   ————————

Providing services 8

If you did not do as well as you hoped in the game, don't despair yet! There are other ways of earning a living than by making and selling manufactured goods. In fact, these days more people are employed in providing services of one kind or another than in making or growing things for sale. What they have for sale is their skill or the use of a special facility of some kind.

Here are some people who provide services:

window cleaners, caretakers, policemen, hairdressers, firemen, civil servants, travel agents, train-drivers, dressmakers, schoolteachers, estate agents, bankers, painters and decorators, solicitors, doctors, footballers, refuse-collectors, actors, taxi-drivers, baby-minders, newspaper delivery boys, telephonists.

If you study this list you will find that the services provided are broadly of two different kinds:

a) Public services, i.e. those provided by local or national government.
b) Private services, i.e. those provided on payment to private individuals or companies.

1   From the list above, see if you can decide which belongs to each category.

When countries grow in prosperity and standards of living rise, the ways in which people spend their money also change. As people get richer they do not want to buy more and more food, or more refrigerators, washing-machines or vacuum cleaners. Instead they begin to spend more on entertainment, health and cosmetic aids, education and holidays. Technological advances and increased leisure time further encourage these developments.

In Britain, for example, out of all those people in employment of any kind, the share of service employment rose from 47% in 1961 to 57% in 1979. It is interesting to note that within this service sector, it was public services that increased most dramatically until 1979. Since then there has been a sharp decline, although the share of the private sector has risen and is expected to continue to do so.

We need to stop and ask some questions at this point.

2   Why should the service industries be growing at such a rate when Britain is not obviously growing in wealth?

3   Why should there be a recent decline in the public sector and yet a

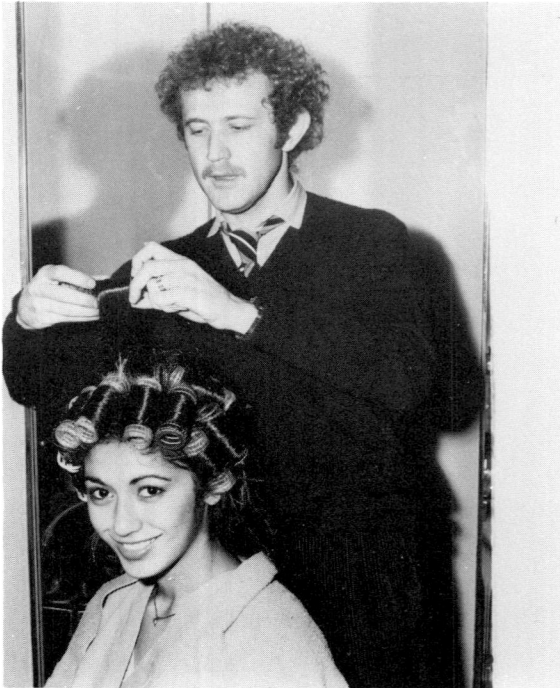

Some examples of direct services to the customer

growth in the private sector, especially in small scale service industries?

4   Are there similar sorts of growth in the service industries of developing countries, such as South Korea or Taiwan?

Discuss these questions with your teacher and see if you can explain some of the apparent contradictions.

Whatever the explanations, there is some real encouragement in the facts for those of you who may be thinking of setting up a small firm which will provide a service direct to the customer.

Much will of course depend upon where you live, whether in town or country, or in a relatively well-off area. It is worth remembering that there may be a very special demand for a high quality service in a more affluent area. For example, a dressmaker is likely to attract more custom with a reputation for style and quality of fit and finish than for cheapness. Wealthy people tend to look for individuality and personal service.

In some respects it may be easier to establish a small firm offering a service than one which manufactures goods. Certainly there will be less outlay on raw materials or components. However, both kinds of enterprise have much in common and you will have to go through similar processes to give your service the best chance of success.

Getting the original idea to start with can be a daunting prospect for some people. Because providing a service is dependent to a large degree on being able to provide a particular skill or knowledge, it is worthwhile writing down the sort of things you like doing and are good at; hobbies especially. Very often a 'brain-storming' session with friends produces the unexpected idea, that is, when a group of people get together and begin by suggesting the first things that come into their minds. Whatever the idea, you will need to do some market research and this will both rationalise and modify the original intention even if it is feasible at all.

You must have tremendous enthusiasm for your idea and possess what business men call 'entrepreneurial drive'. On the other hand, you cannot afford to close your eyes to the financial realities of the situation and you may have to go to your bank manager who will expect you to be aware of the main commitments of the undertaking, which may differ significantly depending upon whether you are setting up, for example, as a window-cleaner or as a hairdresser. In one case you will need no premises (just a home address or telephone number) and relatively little equipment, while in the other you may need a purpose-built salon, special equipment and display.

There are some of the things you will have to consider. There are others and they are sometimes different from the requirements of a small manufacturing firm. Look back at Sections 3 and 5 again.

5   How will you work out what you need to achieve in order to make a profit for your service?

6   Is there a 'break-even' point?

7 What is your productivity dependent upon?

8 How can this be increased?

In Part 2 we shall return to the special problems of manufacturing firms, but whilst analysing these you might like to consider how far they are common to the servicing industry and in what respects they may be different.

Part 2 Expanding the firm

Shall we expand our firm? 9

In Part 1 we considered how we might set up a small manufacturing firm.

Let us assume that we have now done this successfully and we are now wondering whether or not to expand our firm. What do you think are the advantages and disadvantages of expansion? If we decide to expand, how might we do this?

Suppose we decide to expand. We shall have to raise more money to build a larger factory, and one way of doing this would be to turn our private limited company into a public limited company – 'going public' – so that we could raise money on the Stock Exchange. We shall look at this in Section 10.

When we build our larger factory we shall have to consider very carefully where to put it. It is important not only to us but also to the people in the areas where we might build it, and we shall go into this in more detail in Section 11.

A big factory is organised very differently from a small one – for example, in the variety of jobs available. This will be the topic of Section 12.

In a small factory all the workers can easily have direct contact with the managing director – they probably see him every day and know him personally. In a large factory this is not the case, and labour relations have to be organised very carefully. All kinds of difficulties can arise. We shall be looking at some of these in Section 13.

10 'Going public'

10.1 The launching

If we wish to expand our firm, one way of doing this is to change from being a private limited company to being a public limited company so that we can raise more capital by selling shares to the public on The Stock Exchange.

Use either Document 10A or the book supplied by your teacher to obtain the following information.

1 Name a private limited company.

2 Name a public limited company.

3 Why doesn't a company wishing to go public draw up its own prospectus without the aid of a sponsor?

4 Why does the Council of The Stock Exchange check the financial records of a company before allowing it to go public?

5 Why is it made so difficult for companies to go public?

6 What are the four ways of issuing shares? What are the advantages and disadvantages of each method?

7 What is underwriting? Why do companies arrange for the underwriting of their share issues?

8 How do members of the public apply to buy shares in a new public company before it is quoted on The Stock Exchange?

9 Write an introduction to your prospectus, outlining the reasons why your company should go public. Explain particularly why you have chosen to borrow equity rather than fixed-interest capital.

10 Write a letter to the Council of The Stock Exchange explaining why your company should be granted a quotation. Outline the growth potential of your particular company.

11 Imagine you are a journalist. Write an article about the company, outlining the advantages and disadvantages of going public. Show how the directors, the current shareholders, and the workers in the company will be affected.

12 The bulk of the shares in public companies are often owned by so-called institutional shareholders – pension funds, insurance companies, trade unions, etc. Find out what you can about institutional investment.

13 As a shareholder, how can you influence the policy of the company?

10.2 The Stock Exchange

We have seen that one reason for the existence of The Stock Exchange is to enable large companies to raise large amounts of capital from a large number of shareholders, each of whom might contribute only a small proportion of the total capital.

One reason why people buy shares is because every year they can expect to be paid a dividend from the profits which they expect their company to make.

However, very few people would buy shares if they could not sell them again at a later date, and another reason for the existence of The Stock Exchange is to provide this facility.

Use either Document 10B or the book provided by your teacher to answer the following questions.

1 Why is there a branch of The Stock Exchange in many large cities?

2 Why do jobbers specialise in the shares that they handle? Why is it important for jobbers to be in competition with each other?

3 What is the role of stockbrokers on the floor of the Stock Exchange?

4 Explain how share prices are determined on the floor of the Stock Exchange. Why do share prices fluctuate?

5 What is 'the account'? What is the advantage of buying at the beginning of the account?

6 What is meant by (a) the nominal (or face) value of a share and (b) its market value?

10.3 Dividends

When a person buys shares issued by a public company, he becomes one of the owners of that company. This entitles him every year to receive a part of the profits distributed by the company. The payment of part of the profits to shareholders is made by means of the dividend.

For a public company to calculate its dividend, three pieces of information are required:

1 The number of shares (called ordinary shares or equities) issued by the company.

2 The face value of these shares. This is a figure printed on the share certificate which is used for the calculation of dividends. It has nothing at all to do with the market price of the company's shares.

3 The amount of the profit that is to be given out to shareholders.

When this information is available, two simple calculations have to be made:

a) The amount of the profit has to be divided by the number of shares. This tells you how much profit is to be distributed per share.

b) The profit given out per share is expressed as a percentage of the face value of the shares.

For example, the company wishes to give 10p profit per share. The face value of the shares is 20p. The calculation is

$$\frac{10}{20} \times 100 = 50\%$$

The dividend would be 50%.

Example

A company has issued 1 million shares, each with a face value of 25p. It decides to distribute £200000 profit to shareholders. What will be the dividend?

$$\text{Dividend per share} = \frac{200\,000}{1\,000\,000} = £0\cdot20$$

$$\therefore \quad \text{Percentage dividend} = \frac{£0\cdot20}{£0\cdot25} = 80\%$$

Great care has to be taken in this second calculation to make sure that the two figures used are both pounds or both pence. You must not have one figure in pounds and one in pence.

1 Calculate the percentage dividends of companies A, B, and C:

	A	B	C
Number of shares	2 000 000	500 000	1 000 000
Face value of share	20p	20p	50p
Distributed profit	£100 000	£50 000	£20 000

2 I own 500 ordinary shares of £1 each. The dividend is 20% How much shall I receive?

Document 10A *'Going public'*

Imagine that a successful private limited company called ABC Co. Ltd wishes to go public. The rules it must obey are laid down by the Council of The Stock Exchange (see later). ABC Co. Ltd will have to follow this procedure:

a) Its directors must find a *sponsor*. This will usually either be a merchant bank or a firm of stockbrokers. Merchant banks are rather special banks which offer advice and will lend money to large companies. They do not have much to do with ordinary members of the public. Stockbrokers are experts in all matters concerned with shares in public companies.

   The sponsor performs two tasks. He advises ABC Co. Ltd about the rules that have to be obeyed by companies going public, and he investigates ABC Co. Ltd to make sure that it is a reliable and well-run business and is worthy of the privilege of going public.

b) The results of the investigations of the sponsor have to be included in a prospectus. This is a small book that has to be published which tells people who are considering buying shares in ABC Co. Ltd all about the company: the company's history, its directors, its recent sales record, its recent profits, its future prospects – these and other items have to be included.

c) The *Council of The Stock Exchange* checks through the prospectus very carefully before it is published. There is very little about ABC Co. Ltd that the Council will not want to know if it is to allow it to go public. The most important job of the Council is to protect those people who may consider buying shares in ABC Co. Ltd. If ABC Co. Ltd is not a most excellent company then the Council of The Stock Exchange will not give it a quotation.

d) When the Council is sure that ABC Co. Ltd is a sound company, it sets a date for its shares to be available for sale and purchase on The Stock Exchange. ABC Co. Ltd is said to have been 'granted a quotation on The Stock Exchange'.

e) The Sponsor now places advertisements in newspapers encouraging people to buy shares in ABC Co. Ltd. The number of shares to be sold and the price that is to be asked will have been decided, and the task is now to persuade people to invest in the company. As many shares as possible will be sold before the shares are made available for sale on The Stock Exchange; people will buy their shares by filling in an application form and sending off the money. All the money received from the sale of the shares, minus the sponsor's fee and various other costs, will go to ABC Co. Ltd.

Document 10B *The Stock Exchange*

Trading floor of the London Stock Exchange

The most important branch of The Stock Exchange is in London. There are other branches in Glasgow, Liverpool, Manchester, Birmingham, Bristol, Cardiff, Dublin, and Belfast. The Council of The Stock Exchange meets in London, and it is the work of the London Stock Exchange that we will describe.

Every branch of The Stock Exchange is an indoor market. Most people have been to an open-air street market. The stall-holders sell their goods to the people who go to shop. Customers 'shop around' and buy from the stall where the goods are cheapest. Sometimes stall-holders have to lower their prices to sell all their goods.

The sellers in a street market are the stall-holders. The sellers on The Stock Exchange are called *jobbers*. Stall-holders and jobbers do not do exactly the same kind of work. The stall-holder only sells his goods. The jobber buys as well as sells his goods, which are shares. Nevertheless, the jobber and the street-market trader earn their living in a very similar way.

Members of the public are not allowed into that part of The Stock Exchange where the buying and selling of shares takes place. They can-not do their own shopping like customers in a street market. *Stockbrokers* do the actual buying and selling of shares, and anyone who wants to buy shares on The Stock Exchange has to have a stockbroker.

The work of The Stock Exchange proceeds as follows. Jobbers are free to buy and sell shares at any price they like. Stockbrokers are free to deal with any jobber that they like. Competition between jobbers ensures that prices are fair. Jobbers who ask unreasonably high prices when they try to sell shares will find that they do no business. Jobbers who offer very low prices when stockbrokers try to sell to them will suffer a similar fate.

Stockbrokers 'shop around' to obtain the best possible prices for their clients. If they are selling shares, they obtain the highest price possible. If they are buying shares, they go to the jobber selling at the lowest price.

No money changes hands when stockbrokers and jobbers do business. Both make a note of the deal that they have made, and all exchanges of money take place later. Stockbrokers and jobbers trust one another completely – that is why the motto of The Stock Exchange is, 'My word is my bond.'

Jobbers and stockbrokers thus decide between them the prices of all shares bought and sold on The Stock Exchange. The companies whose shares are being bought and sold have no say at all in deciding their price. The price that any share will fetch on The Stock Exchange is called its *market price*.

How do jobbers and stockbrokers earn a living? Jobbers always try to sell shares for more money than they had to pay for them. The difference between the buying and selling prices is called the 'jobber's turn'. It is usually quite small, a matter of a few pence per share, and it is the income of the jobber. The stockbroker charges his customers a fee on small transactions. Often it is a percentage of the value of this transaction, usually $1\frac{1}{4}\%$. Thus, if shares worth £1000 are bought for a client by a stockbroker, his fee would be £12·50.

Where shall we build our new factory? 11

11.1 Factors affecting our choice

If a firm finds it necessary to expand because of increasing sales, the directors may decide to enlarge their existing factory. However, this is often impossible because no adjoining land is available, and they must decide on a new site for the larger factory.

In making their decision, the directors will try to choose a site where the costs are as low as possible, and the following factors must be taken into account.

1 The source of raw material or components, and the location of the market

When manufacturing a product, a firm must obtain suitable raw materials and components, but it must also transport the finished products to their final selling point or market. Often the market and the source of raw materials or components are in different places. In this case the businessman must choose whether to situate his factory near the source of the raw materials, near the market, or somewhere in-between. When making the decision he will try to choose a point where his overall transport costs are lowest. He has either to manufacture the product at the site of the raw materials and transport the final product to the market, or to move the raw materials to the market and manufacture the product there.

The costs of transport are mainly determined by the bulk or volume of the product. Where bulky raw materials are involved, the production process may reduce their volume and thus reduce transport costs. Products of this type are said to be 'bulk-reducing', and their manufacture usually takes place at the site of the raw material.

Other types of products, however, increase in bulk or volume during the manufacturing process and are therefore relatively expensive to transport in their final stage. These products are said to be 'bulk-increasing', and their manufacture tends to be situated near the market.

Which of the following products are bulk-increasing and which bulk-reducing in their manufacture?

a) Metal boxes
b) Furniture
c) Steel manufacture
d) Bread
e) Lemonade
f) Canning of peas

Are there any industries in your area which are bulk-increasing or bulk-reducing?

2 Transport

What are the possible methods of transport for our raw materials and finished products? What developments in recent years have made transport from one part of the country to another easier?

Will access to transport facilities be an important factor in determining the location of our factory? Consider two different cases: (a) where we have a few large customers widely distributed, (b) where we distribute direct to many small shops.

3 Cost of land

The firm can either buy or rent the land it requires. Land varies in cost from place to place. Where would you expect to find the most expensive land? Why would it be so expensive?

The importance of the cost of land will vary from industry to industry. If a factory requires a lot of land the firm will need to find cheap land, but if the factory can be relatively small (compared to the price of the product) the firm may decide to use more expensive land in order to have access to other amenities.

In which of the following industries do you consider that the cost of land would be relatively important?

a) Motor-car manufacturing   d) Bread baking
b) Shoe manufacturing   e) Steel manufacturing
c) Radio manufacturing   f) Cloth weaving

4 Power

Make a list of all the possible sources of power for driving the machinery in a factory.

Prior to 1920, the most readily available source of power was coal. If we had chosen this as our source of power, in what regions should we have built our factory? Why?

Why do we have a wider choice of location for our factory today than we would have had in 1920?

A few industries use very large amounts of power and may need to be located near the source of power. Can you name one of these?

5 Labour with appropriate skills

In many cases, firms require workers with certain specific types of skills, and the availability of those workers varies from area to area of the country.

One important reason for this is connected with the decline of industries. When a particular type of industry has become established in an area, other firms of the same nature tend to cluster in the same locality (see Section 5). If the demand for the product of this industry declines, then workers are available to be employed by a growing industry requiring similar skills. Thus the decline of shipbuilding industry in a particular area would make available workers with metal-working skills.

1   What are the reasons why similar firms tend to cluster in the same locality?

2   Plot the following towns on an outline map of Great Britain, and use the book 'Britain: an official handbook' to discover the main industries of each:

1	Coventry	7	Stoke-on-Trent
2	Luton	8	Leicester
3	Southampton	9	Bolton
4	Bristol	10	Bradford
5	Ipswich	11	Newcastle-upon-Tyne
6	Birmingham	12	Glasgow

3   Documents 11A and 11B show how the number of people engaged in various industries changed between 1923 and 1938 and between 1951 and 1979.

Can you think of any reasons why certain industries declined and others expanded during each of these two periods?

What general trends or patterns are indicated by the figures in Document 11B?

4   Where are the main problems being created today by declining industries?

5   What action, if any, is the Government taking in the various areas?

6.   Other factors

In the past, the economic factors we have been discussing were not as important as they are today in determining the location of particular industries. Many centres of industry owe their origin to 'other factors' – from simple explanations like 'it just so happened' that the person who set it up lived there, that there was some accommodation available there, etc., to more complicated explanations like a group of persecuted foreign immigrants settled there and brought their skills with them. Whatever the case, as we shall see in Section 11.2, once an industry has become established in an area, other similar firms tend to go to there as well.

For thirty years after the Second World War government policy was an important factor in determining the location of certain industries. It is generally recognised today, however, that such policies can only be partially successful at best, and with rapid developments in high technology, communication and information channels, they are likely to be less influential than some other factors. For example, the so-called 'Green Field' sites of developing towns like Milton Keynes, Peterborough and Northampton are relatively cheap to acquire, and in addition these areas have good communications and a reputation for excellent labour relations. Imagine also the effects that the opening up of a Channel Tunnel would have on industrial growth in East Kent.

11.2 Making our choice

Read Document 11C, which examines some of the reasons why the Ford Motor Company factory is located at Dagenham.

Your teacher will now divide the class into groups. Each group elects a chairman and secretary and one director to be responsible for each of the factors which influence choice of location (see Section 11.1). Each group decides the best location for a fairly large factory manufacturing:

1   petroleum products,
2   motor cars,
3   furniture,
4   plastic kitchen equipment.

Document 11A　*Industrial distribution of employment in the United Kingdom, 1923-38*

Industry	Estimated number of insured persons aged 16 to 64 in employment in June 1938	Percentage increase (+) or decrease (−) since June 1923
Expanding:		
Distributive trades	1 911 218	+ 64·5
Building and contracting	1 141 203	+ 63·2
General engineering	591 430	+ 16·8
Hotel, restaurant, etc., service	394 877	+ 71·7
Road transport	385 312	+ 73·1
Motor and aircraft engineering	360 836	+109·4
Local government service	317 323	+ 49·8
Electrical manufacturing	275 120	+128·7
Printing, publishing and bookbinding	268 564	+ 27·6
Gas, water and electricity supply	205 177	+ 34·2
Tailoring	190 776	+ 8·5
Laundries, dyeing, etc.	168 629	+ 69·5
Professional services	165 608	+ 61·7
Bread, biscuit and cake-making	163 446	+ 15·7
Furniture making	132 422	+ 57·3
Entertainments, sport, etc.	127 731	+150·5
Contracting:		
Coal mining	701 713	− 41·5
Cotton manufacturing	251 184	− 43·2
Woollen and worsted manufacturing	164 731	− 32·3
Iron and steel	152 965	− 17·7
Railway service (non-permanent workers)	149 508	− 14·0
Shipbuilding	139 968	− 4·8
Dock, harbour, etc. service	118 270	− 14·6
Boot and shoe manufacturing	111 792	− 11·9
All industries	12 075 268	+ 21·5

* *Ministry of Labour Gazette*, December 1938, pp. 486, 487.

Document 11B *Industrial distribution of employment in the United Kingdom, 1951–79*

	1951	1961	1966	1974	1977	1979
Agriculture, forestry and fishing	1126	855	762	404	388	366 (thousands)
Mining and quarrying	841	722	561	347	350	337
Food, drink and tobacco	727	704	743	740	711	699
Chemicals and allied industries	435	499	493	432	473	475
Metal manufacture	616	626	588	506	483	450
Engineering and electrical goods	1601	2031	2185	1953	1829	1802
Shipbuilding and marine engineering	277	237	178	175	182	172
Vehicles	735	838	809	783	750	751
Other metal goods	458	525	562	577	535	525
Textiles	986	790	721	546	512	480
Leather, leather goods and fur	78	60	59	42	41	39
Clothing and footwear	676	546	515	404	388	380
Bricks, pottery and glass, etc.	314	321	329	295	264	260
Timber, furniture, etc.	326	304	299	277	258	259
Paper, printing and publishing	515	605	617	582	537	543
Other manufacturing industries	264	295	327	350	331	321
Construction	1388	1600	1880	1290	1270	1294
Gas, electricity, water	357	377	411	337	347	354
Transport and communication	1704	1673	1608	1483	1468	1482
Distributive trades	2689	3189	3245	2707	2753	2805
Insurance, banking, finance	435	572	656	1101	1145	1199
Professional and scientific services	1524	2120	2499	3284	3646	3719
Others, miscellaneous	3485	3519	3871	3682	3957	4104
Total:	21 557	23 010	23 918	22 297	22 619	22 815

Source: Annual Abstract of Statistics, Central Statistical Office.

Document 11C The Ford Motor Company, Dagenham

The Ford Motor Company of the United States purchased 294 acres of land at Dagenham in 1924, including a water-front on the River Thames, for £150000. The first vehicle was produced on the site in 1931.

The site was away from the centre of London and there was plenty of cheap and relatively flat land available for future expansion. Today the site consists of 665 acres. The wharf facilities on the River Thames will accommodate ships of 15000 tons. This enables the easy import of raw materials of about 14500 tons a day. In 1972, 274 ships and nearly 1000 barges docked to unload raw materials such as iron ore and coal, and to ship out vehicles and spare parts. These are exported down the River Thames to Europe and the rest of the world. The company's blast furnace and power station provide the factory with some of its own steel and electricity, and the River Thames provides plenty of water for cooling purposes.

In the 1950's the London County Council was building a very large housing estate on the outskirts of what was then Dagenham Village. The workers who moved into these houses provided the company with a ready supply of suitably skilled labour. Today the Dagenham works employs some 21000 people.

12 How is a big factory different from a small one?

When we have raised the money to expand our business, and decided where to locate our new factory, we must plan it in a very different way from our original small works. The reasons for this will become clear when we make a detailed study of a medium-sized factory.

Read through Document 12A, 'The Northern Domestic Appliance Co. Ltd', then refer back to Section 5 and read through the document on the Wyre Co. Ltd. We shall be making some comparisons between the two factories.

Now answer the following questions.

1   How many directors does the Northern Domestic Appliance Co. Ltd have? Make a list of the departments in the company for which each director is responsible.

2   What duties are performed by the personnel-and-training department?

3   Make a list of five people in the firm who do jobs similar to those in the Wyre Co. Ltd. Make another list of five people who have no counterpart in the smaller firm. Why should the larger firm require the skills of workers of this type, but not the smaller firm?

4   What training and career experience would each of the following require: (a) the chief work-study engineer, (b) the purchasing manager, (c) the financial director, (d) the senior shop steward?

5   Draw a 'flow diagram' of the production line of the factory. Start your diagram by showing the raw materials and components as they enter the factory, and finish it by showing the completed goods leaving the factory.

6   What influence might the shop stewards in the factory have over the organisation and running of the production line? How might the management of the company make use of the experience and advice of the shop stewards to make the production line run efficiently?

7   Seven different trade unions have members employed by the company, and we are told that 'the wage-bargaining procedure is somewhat complex'. What does this mean? Make a list of all the difficulties that might be created for both management and workers by the existence of so many unions.

8 The Wyre Co. Ltd would have to stop work if there were strikes in the firms which produced wire, electroplating, or electric power. Make a list of the industries on which the Northern Domestic Appliance Co. Ltd is reliant. Is this firm more or less in danger from strikes in other factories than the Wyre Co. Ltd?

9 What welfare and social facilities are available to the workers in the larger firm which are not available in the smaller firm? Can you think of any reasons why a worker might prefer to join a works social club rather than a club in the district where he lives?

10 Suppose a simple new process were to be invented for giving metal a cheap, durable ceramic coat suitable for cookers, and the firm decided to introduce this instead of enamelling. Describe how you might view this change from the point of view of (a) the director of manufacturing, (b) a worker in the enamelling department.

11 In Section 5 we saw that small firms have the advantage of flexibility – they can change the production line relatively easily to do short runs of production. What is the corresponding advantage of large firms? Document 12B may help you.

12 In the Wyre Co. Ltd, which is a private company, the managing director, Mr Wyre, has a substantial portion of the shares and therefore receives a substantial portion of the profits. The company we are now studying is a public company with a much greater number of shares owned by a large number of different people. The managing director and the other four working directors own some shares, but most of their income is made up from their salaries as executive directors: if the firm makes higher profits, most of the money goes to the other shareholders.

Presumably Mr Wyre's aim is to make as much profit as possible. If you were a working director of the Northern Domestic Appliance Co. Ltd, would your aims be in any way different?

13 The Northern Domestic Appliance Co. Ltd faces strong competition from other firms making similar products. What effect might this competition have on (a) the prices it charges, (b) the quality of the goods it produces?

14 What steps might the Northern Domestic Appliance Co. Ltd take to increase demand for its products?

15 How might the decisions mentioned in questions 10 and 14 be taken within the firm? Think about who might have the idea, and who would be concerned in each of these decisions.

16 When the present recession began to affect sales, what steps would you have taken, as managing director, to increase production?

17 When it came to making workers redundant, how would you have wanted to agree with the unions that this should take place? 'Last in, first out?'

Document 12A *The Northern Domestic Appliance Co. Ltd*

This is a public company with an issued ordinary-share capital of £750 000. The shares are widely distributed among shareholders, and no one shareholder has more than £10 000 worth. The turnover is about £5 million. Until recently there were about 1000 employees, but it is now reduced to 700. The firm, like many others, hopes that this recession will pass and that they will be able to return to the previous level of production. This document therefore describes the firm as it was at full production and the changes caused by the recession are discussed at the end.

The company produce mainly cookers and fires. The raw materials are iron castings (the foundry is a subsidiary company), sheet steel, and a very wide variety of bought-in components such as thermostats, wooden surrounds for fires, wire shelves, knobs, nuts and bolts, etc.

The home market for domestic appliances is very competitive, because in the showrooms of the gas board and the electricity board a customer has the opportunity to compare the products of many manufacturers. The firm must therefore try to produce cookers and fires which are better than those of its rivals at a price which is the same or slightly lower. They therefore employ three research-and-development teams (cookers, fires, and future products) consisting of scientists and engineers and their assistants, about 25 people in all, whose job it is to design the required product. They work in close co-operation with draughtsmen in the design department (about 18 people) under the general direction of the technical manager, who is in turn responsible to the technical director.

If they come up with a design which has

Figure 12A. Plan of factory of the Northern Domestic Appliance Co. Ltd

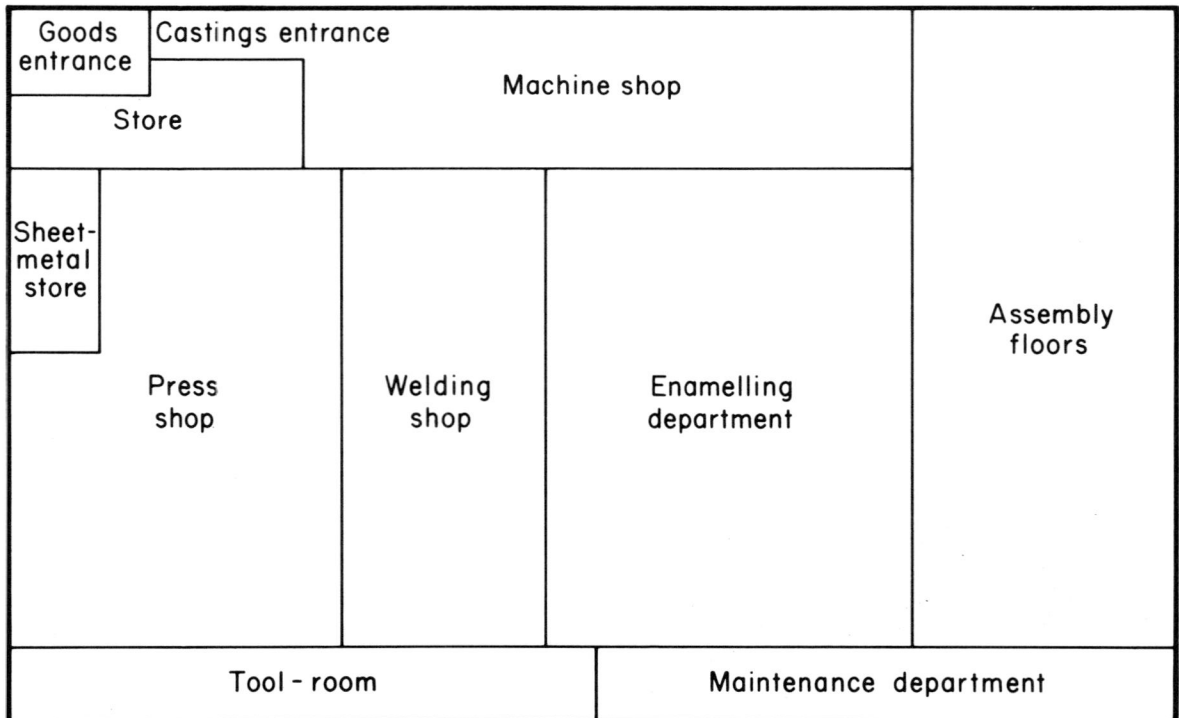

possibilities, then the marketing executive carries out market research to find out what the demand will be, and if the product appears to have a good sale then a production line is organised.

The production-planning department decides how the product will be made and organises the flow of work through the factory. The purchasing department makes arrangements for the purchase of raw material and components. Usually the details are put on the firm's computer (at present an ICL 1901) so that immediately an order is received the computer will work out how many of each component needs to be ordered. The tool-room (about 30 highly skilled technicians) produces the jigs and tools. The planning and purchasing departments, the tool-room, and the factory itself come under the manufacturing director.

Refer now to figure 12A, the plan of the factory. Sheet steel, castings, and bought-in components come in and are inspected. Castings pass to the machine shop, where milling and drilling takes place. Some of this work must be done to very close tolerances, and about 8 of the men in this department are highly skilled, whereas the other 30 are only semi-skilled and require relatively little training. The finished castings pass to the assembly floors.

The sheet steel passes first to the press shop, where it is guillotined to size and stamped into shape. The smaller parts are done in hand presses, worked mainly by women, and the larger parts are stamped by powerful hydraulic presses worked by men. Altogether there are 75 people in this department. Any parts which require electroplating are sent out to a specialist firm.

The pressed steel parts then go into the welding shop, where they are assembled on jigs and fixed together by electric spot welding. About 20 men work in this department.

After inspection and correction of faults, the parts are cleaned and degreased, given a carbon coating, and then enamelled by hand-dipping or spraying. They are then dried, inspected, and baked in ovens through which they pass on a conveyor line. About 90 men and women work in this department. After inspection, the parts pass to the assembly floors.

There are separate assembly lines for the cookers and the fires, employing about 160 people in all. There is an extensive overhead conveyor system to get all the parts from the stores to the various parts of the factory where they are required, including the final assembly line. After assembly, there is extensive inspection before the product is packed for transportation.

The foremen of the machine shop, press shop, and welding shop are responsible to the assistant works manager, who together with the managers of the enamelling department and the assembly floor is responsible to the works manager. The production-control department is responsible for chasing the progress of work through the factory, and the work-study engineers are responsible for tasks such as improving the flow of work through the factory and fixing the standard times for jobs. The works manager, the production controller, and the chief work-study engineer are responsible to the manufacturing director, as is also the maintenance department. The inspectors, of whom there are over 50, are responsible to the technical director. The transport department comes under the marketing director.

There are four main sections of the accounts office. One section deals with the accounts for raw materials and components – the 'bought ledger' – another deals with the 'sales ledger', and a third deals with wages. All these three sections, about 50 people in all, are responsible to the chief accountant, who is in turn responsible to the financial director (who is also the company secretary). The fourth section is the computer section: the systems analyst and the programmers and operators work under the data-processing manager, who is again responsible to the financial director. The security department is also responsible to the financial director.

The hiring and training of all employees is the responsibility of the personnel-and-training department, the head of which reports directly to the chief executive.

A sample of employees gave the following descriptions of their careers.

A spot welder

Short on-the-job training.

A tool-room craftsman

Joined the firm at 16+ with five good grades in CSE subjects. The first year was full-time at the college of further education, followed by three years further training with day release.

An assembly-line operator

Joined the firm as a married woman. Received a few weeks training in the firm's 'school'.

(The firm had introduced this schooling period because before this there had been a high rate of turnover among assembly-line operators during their first few weeks of employment.)

A junior secretary

Joined the firm at 16+ with five GCE O-levels including English. Had taken day release to follow a typing and commercial-studies course, and had made junior secretary by the age of 20.

Section manager 'sales ledger'

Left school at 16+ with four GCE O-levels, had then taken a two-year OND Business Studies (now BEC Diploma) course at the college of further education and joined the firm at 18+ as a ledger clerk. His OND gave him exemption from part of the Institute of Cost and Works Accountants examination, and he had taken the rest of the examination by spare-time study over a period of four years. (The minimum period is five years from the age of 16+, but few people pass every stage the first time.) He was earning over £7000 per annum by the age of 30 (in 1980).

Technical manager

A good honours graduate in physics who took a post-graduate apprenticeship with a firm of heating engineers. Later he did research and development with another manufacturer of domestic appliances, and he also spent some time as a marketing executive.

Works manager

Left school at 18+ with two A-levels (physics and chemistry) and did a student apprenticeship, after which he took a four-year sandwich course at the local polytechnic to give him a CNAA degree in engineering. After being in charge of the machine shop for some time, he transferred to production control, and he then had a period in work study with another firm. He came back as assistant works manager, and later succeeded as works manager.

It is the aim of the personnel department to ensure that there are always one or two people being 'groomed' to succeed to each post in middle or senior management. For example, if the production controller is due to retire in three or four years time, one or two of the work-study engineers might be sent on production-control courses and then given the necessary experience, even if it meant creating a post of assistant production controller (in parallel with the deputy production controller, who is an older man due to retire himself a few years after the controller).

About 80% of the workers are members of the General and Municipal Workers' Union. The other 20% belong to a variety of unions – Transport and General Workers' Union (TGWU), the Amalgamated Union of Engineering Workers (AUEW), the draughtsmen's union TASS, and the Association of Scientific, Technical and Managerial Staff (ASTMS).

There being such a variety of different jobs, the wage-bargaining procedure is somewhat complex, as in the rest of the engineering industry. A group of workers who are dissatisfied with the rate they are receiving for a particular job might take the following course of action. The bargaining would stop at the stage when both workers and management were satisfied that a fair solution had been reached.

a) Workers discuss their dissatisfaction with their foreman.
b) Workers and the shop steward of their union talk to the foreman.
c) The shop steward talks to the foreman and the departmental manager.
d) The shop steward and the factory convenor (the chairman of the committee of the shop stewards from all the unions in the factory) talk to the departmental manager and the personnel manager.
e) The factory convenor talks to the personnel manager and the director.
f) The factory convenor and the union district organiser talk to the director and officials from the employers' federation.

The firm has an extensive range of welfare and social services. There is a surgery with a full-time nurse, and there is a works canteen and a staff canteen which serve subsidised meals. There is a social club which has two dance halls, facilities for indoor games, bars, and playing fields.

All matters other than those concerning pay can be discussed at meetings of the Joint Consultative Committee, which consists of five representatives of the workers and five representatives of the management, under the chairmanship of the personnel manager.

This describes the firm as it was until 1979. Since then there has been a recession so that people have bought fewer cookers and fires. The firm has cut production and made about 300 workers redundant.

Document 12B   *Percentage of total sales of various commodities accounted for by the five leading firms in each trade*

Commodity	Percentage	Commodity	Percentage
Bread	70	Bedding	33
Bacon	31	Pottery	45
Sugar	99	Cutlery	45
Margarine	97	Pharmaceuticals	34
Soap and Detergents	78	Paint	47
Beer	56	Wallpaper	92
Tobacco goods	99	Watches and Clocks	82
Footwear	28	Radios	78
Hosiery and knitted goods	36	Domestic electrical goods	60
Leather goods	16	Motor Vehicles	70
Women's outer clothes	17	Agricultural Machinery	31
Furniture	12		

13 'What about *my* share of the profits?'

13.1 Joining a trade union

In a firm with about fifty workers, many of them will know the managing director as a person, and negotiations over wages, conditions of work, etc. can often be conducted face-to-face. In the much larger firm, however, the relations between management and workers are usually much more complicated.

Imagine that you are a worker in a large firm, and you get to know that the firm has substantially increased its profits. You and your workmates naturally decide that you would like some of the increased profits as increased wages.

There are three groups of workers in the firm, and their basic weekly wages are as follows:

skilled workers (e.g. maintenance engineers), £110;
semi-skilled workers (e.g. assembly-line workers), £90;
unskilled workers (e.g. packers, cleaners), £80.

There is a shortage of skilled and semi-skilled workers in the area, but a number of unemployed unskilled workers. The employers say that they intend to pay increased wages to the skilled and semi-skilled workers, but nothing more to the unskilled workers.

Your teacher will divide you into three groups representing each of the groups of workers in the factory.

Discuss what you are going to do about the wage offer.

In order to protect your position you may decide to join a trade union. There are three types of union which you must consider:

an *industry union*, which seeks to represent all the workers in a particular industry whatever their type of job;
a *craft union*, which represents a particular kind of skilled worker whichever industry he may be in;
a *general union*, which represents semi-skilled and unskilled workers doing many different kinds of jobs in a wide variety of industries.

Examine Document 13A. Decide which are (a) industry unions, (b) craft unions, (c) general unions.

What is a 'white collar' union?

In most factories there are members of more than one union. For example, the Ford Motor Co. has to deal with fifteen unions in their pay negotiations. If there is more than one union in a factory, this is referred to as 'multiunionism'.

What problems do you think multiunionism might cause in a factory?

What are the benefits of multiunionism to the workers?

From the literature provided by your teacher, make a list of the benefits provided by trade unions.

In most European countries there are 'dirty jobs' which the Europeans do not want to do themselves and which are done by 'guest workers' from other countries. For example, thousands of men from Turkey do unskilled jobs in West Germany, sending money home to their families in Turkey. Most of these men live in hostels. Very few belong to trade unions.

What difficulties could arise from this situation?

13.2 The organisational structure of a trade union

1 The factory floor

The workers in a particular union in each part of the factory are represented by a shop steward. He is elected by the workers each year and, although he continues with his job, he devotes much of his time to his duties as shop steward. He looks after all the interests of the workers and helps to solve any problems they may have in the factory.

Much of his time is taken up 'trouble-shooting', e.g. a worker may object to being moved by the foreman from one job to another and the shop steward will be called in to represent the worker in discussions with the management.

In very large factories, one senior shop steward will act as convenor of meetings for all the shop stewards from that union, and there may be a convenor of meetings for all the shop stewards from all the unions represented in the firm. The shop stewards and management frequently work out together the application of wage negotiations agreed at national level.

In most large firms, representatives of management and shop stewards meet from time to time as a Consultative Committee to discuss matters such as conditions of work, safety regulations, social facilities, and dates of holidays.

1 Write an imaginary diary of a day in the life of a shop steward.

2 The structure of a union

This varies from one union to another, but the following is fairly typical.

From time to time members of a union in a particular area will meet together – the branch or 'lodge' meeting. This local meeting will elect representatives to a district committee. Sometimes the local lodge or district has a permanent headquarters and paid full-time staff.

The local lodge or district elects representatives to the national committee, which usually has a full-time president and general secretary. The national committee is the most powerful force in controlling the affairs of the union, and many national presidents and secretaries are well known names.

A local branch union
meeting

The national committee elects representatives to the general council of the Trades Union Congress (TUC).

The local branch also elects representatives to a local district meeting of all trade unions – the Trades Council – which in turn elects representatives to a national Federation of Trades Councils.

The annual meeting of the
Trades Union Congress
(Andrew Wiard, *Report*)

RECONSTRU   AIN - JOBS FOR YOUTH -

2 Draw a diagram representing clearly the structure of a union and its various connections with other organisations.

3 The Trades Union Congress and the Confederation of British Industry

Most trade unions in Britain are affiliated to the Trades Union Congress (TUC), which therefore represents some eleven million members. The TUC represents the trade-union movement in discussions with the government, employers, and unions overseas.

Employers too have their organisations, usually on an industrial basis, e.g. many of the employers in the engineering industry belong to the Engineering Employers Association. These associations too have district and national committees. Most employers associations are affiliated to the Confederation of British Industries (CBI) which represents the employers' point of view in talks with government, trade unions, and other organisations.

3 Suppose a government minister wished to introduce legislation in Parliament to make it compulsory for firms to give details of their costs and profits to their employees. What discussions would probably take place before drafting the Bill for Parliament?

4 Wage negotiations

In most industries, wage negotiations are very complicated.

Many industries have a Joint National Council which consists of representatives of the union national committees and representatives of the national committee of the appropriate employers association. The Joint National Council negotiates a basic wage structure which is further modified by negotiations at factory level.

A member of your local Trades Council can be invited to the school to talk to you, and you should question him in detail about machinery for negotiating wages and settling disputes.

You can then write an account of the machinery which is used in an important local industry.

13.3 Industrial disputes

In all industries, differences of opinion occur between workers and management and among the workers themselves. Some of these differences concern pay, but many are concerned with other matters, such as the number of men required to operate a machine, or alleged victimisation.

In many factories a 'disputes procedure' has been established whereby a problem is discussed by trade-union and management representatives at a number of levels until a solution is found. If a solution is not found easily, the workers may take some form of industrial action.

Imagine that you work in a factory where a dispute has occurred over the manning of a new machine. Six men were required to man the old machine, but the manager maintains that only four men are required for the new machine. The workers object.

Divide into groups to discuss the way in which the problem might be dealt with. If, as workers, you are not happy about the solution proposed, what forms of industrial action might you take?

Sometimes disputes lead to strike action. If the strike has the support of the union headquarters it is called an 'official' strike, but if the men stop work without union support the strike is called 'unofficial'.

From the workers' point of view, many factors will affect the likely success of a strike. Ideally, the workers should have official union support, be united, have sufficient union funds to pay strike pay over a long period if necessary, and provide a product or service the lack of which will produce immediate hardship to a large number of people.

Document 13B gives the background to two industrial disputes. Discuss whether the workers are likely to be successful in achieving their demands.

The effects of industrial action can be widespread. What would be the effects of the disputes described in Document 13B.

Document 13C shows the strike record of this country and compares it with that of other countries.

Can you account for the changes in the number of days lost through strikes in Britain?

Can you account for the relative strike records of various countries?

13.4 Industrial-relations problems

From watching TV news items and from the work you did on previous sections of this course you will have learnt something about the kind of disputes which can arise in industry.

It is important that we should learn to look at problems from several different points of view, so in each of the following case studies you will act out a different part. When you have been told which character you will act, try to think yourself into being that person, and behave in the discussion as you think he or she would behave.

Case 1 A question of commission

Characters: Van driver
                Union district organiser
                Shopkeeper
                Managing director of bread company

Background to the case

The workers in question are van drivers who sell bread and cakes to shops. They earn a basic wage plus a commission based on sales. The more they sell, the more they earn. It has been the practice of the bread company to accept back unsold bread without charge. The cost of producing bread is rising, so the makers decide to charge the shopkeepers the full price for bread whether it is sold or unsold.

Shopkeepers have to be more careful, and order less bread. The take-home pay of the bread salesmen falls. The union district organiser demands that the management increase the men's basic wage to compensate for the loss of commission. The management refuse, saying that the present wage agreement has another year to run. The men come out on official strike.

Van driver. My wages have dropped by nearly £5 per week. I have a wife and two children to support, and £5 is a lot of money to me. The management caused the trouble by refusing to sell bread on a sale-or-return basis. My wages are being sacrificed to increase their profits, and I am prepared to stay out on strike for a long time to obtain the extra money.

Union district organiser. The management did not consult me at all when they changed their arrangements for selling bread, yet they must have known that it would cost my members money. I was suspicious about the idea of payment by commission in the first place, and I intend to obtain a high basic wage for my members as soon as possible. The management must learn to take the union more seriously.

Shopkeeper. I am receiving no bread at present, and I am in danger of going bankrupt. I have told the bread manufacturers that I will buy bread from another bakery if this drags on much longer, and I know some other shopkeepers who will do the same. The bread manufacturers were right to refuse to accept back unsold bread, because it did encourage wasteful ordering, but the union should have been consulted. Why should the van drivers suffer a drop in pay?

Bread manufacturer. It is true that we have made a mess of our labour relations here. We should have consulted the union. However, I object strongly to the union telling us what to do. I also suspect that they want to get rid of the commission element in the men's wages and want a high basic wage instead. This I will not accept. I am willing to compromise because I am losing business, but there are matters of principle at stake here which I don't intend to sacrifice.

Case 2 An unofficial strike

Characters: A worker
            Shop steward
            Union district organiser

Background to the case

A dispute arose because a worker was moved from one department to another against his will. The union district organiser told the men to keep calm until he had settled the case with the management, but the shop steward was put under pressure by the worker who had been moved, a mate of his, and he called an unofficial one-day strike. A few of the workers did not come out on strike, and afterwards the shop steward and the other workers claimed that these workers ought to pool the money they had earned on that day with the workers who *had* come out. Most of the non-strikers agreed, but one of them objected to union headquarters. There is now to be a discussion between the worker who objected, the shop steward, and the union district organiser.

The worker. My wife has just had a baby, and I cannot afford to lose any money. The whole thing could have been settled by the union and, if the man who was moved hadn't happened to be a mate of the shop steward, there would never have been a strike. I am going to hang on to my pay, but I want the district organiser to know all about it to make sure I don't get victimised in the future.

Shop steward. This lad's a troublemaker. If I don't make him knuckle under on this one, I shall look a right fool and there's no telling the trouble I may have in future.

Union district organiser. The lad's in the right, but what good will it do if he persists? The other workers may get their own back on him later, and I shall be at cross-purposes with the shop steward and the workers who went on strike. Perhaps the best thing I can do is to say, 'The strike was unofficial, settle it among yourselves.'

Case 3 A demarcation dispute

Characters: Shop steward of the general union
                Full-time official of the general union
                Shop steward of the craft union
                Full-time official of the craft union
                Work-study engineer
                Works manager

Background to the case

At this particular firm, all skilled work with plastics is done by members of a craft union, but packaging is done by members of a general union. Packaging normally consists of just wrapping the products in plastic sheet, but the firm are now starting to export to a country with a humid climate, and they have decided that the plastic bags must be heat-sealed. The management and the general union are happy that this job should be done by the packaging workers, but the craft workers' union are claiming that this is a skilled job and their workers must be introduced into the packaging department to operate the heat-sealing machine.

Shop steward and full-time official of the general union. The packaging department is a 'closed shop' for our union, and we would like to keep it that way. This job isn't really as skilled as the jobs the craft workers normally do, and our men could easily do it. But because it is a little more skilled than the normal packaging, we shall be able to get higher rates of pay than usual for it, and in future negotiations we shall be able to edge up these rates to approach those of the craft workers (after all, they are now claiming it is a craft worker's job). Then we shall be able to edge up the rates of pay of the rest of the packaging workers on the grounds that the differentials must not be allowed to grow too large. There is a lot in this case for us.

Shop steward and full-time official of the craft union. This job isn't as skilled as the jobs our men normally do, and to that extent we are demeaning ourselves by taking it on. On the other hand, as these new materials are introduced we have had to fight hard to keep our hold on the skilled jobs, and if we let this one go there is no telling where it will end. Surely we can persuade our brothers in the general union that it does no good to the workers as a whole to let the management get away with paying general rates for this job.

Management team. It suits us to have the packaging department as a closed shop – we have only one union to deal with. If we let in another union, there will be no end to the demarcation disputes. Also, we don't see why we should pay craft rates for a job which isn't all that skilled.

Case 4 A question of promotion

Characters: Skilled worker
           Graduate trainee
           Shop steward
           Full-time union official
           Personnel officer
           Works manager
           Managing director

Background to the case

This firm have in the past recruited their foremen from among their skilled workers, and for the present vacancy there is a suitable candidate among these workers. He is very good at his job, he is respected by his fellow workers, and he would probably make a good foreman. However, he has no educational qualifications, and he probably wouldn't get any higher than foreman.

There is another man in the firm who is a graduate engineer and came in as a graduate trainee. He has done the training specified by the Industrial Training Board, and worked on the shop floor for a short time. He is a member of the same trade union. He is good at his job, and popular with the workers. The union have known all about him, but thought this was a new and better way of getting experience on the way to one of the 'professional' posts such as production-planning engineer or assistant departmental manager. They are dismayed to find him coming in as foreman, and they have objected strongly.

Skilled worker. I would quite like to be a foreman, but I am not very bothered. The pay isn't very different, and the responsibility is much greater. I am certainly not going to swot for any exams to get the job. The other chap's all right. Why all the fuss?

Graduate trainee. I would have liked one of the 'professional' jobs, but there are a lot more graduates about these days, and this is a step in the right direction. I am sorry for the other man, but that's life.

Shop steward. They are both OK by me and the rest of the workers. Who wants to be foreman, anyway?

Full-time official. There aren't many chances of promotion for our men, and it's important to keep them open. This graduate's all right, but he isn't really one of 'us'. Anyway, the non-graduate's got more experience, and the important thing is whether you can do the job, not whether you've got a bit of paper.

Management team. We must make it quite clear that we can promote who we like to whatever job we like, and this is a good case in which to establish the principle. Foremen jobs are becoming a great deal more responsible, and it will suit us very well if we can get into these jobs some sound and popular men with a wider horizon than the usual foreman: someone who when it comes to a crunch will be on our side, not the workers'.

Case 5 Consultation

Characters: Personnel manager, acting as chairman of consultation committee
Four representatives of management
Four representatives of workers

Background to the case

The firm has gradually increased in size, and there have been a number of troubles which could have been avoided if the workers had been fully aware of all the reasons for the decisions which were made. The management have therefore established this consultation committee, which can discuss all matters except those relating to pay. It is not yet clear whether this committee is only advisory, or whether all their findings will be acted upon.

Recently the workers in one department agreed to shorten their lunch break so that they could leave earlier in the afternoon. The workers' representatives on this committee are now claiming that this matter should have been referred to this committee before a decision was taken.

Workers' representative. If this committee is to do any good, we must make sure that all matters of this sort are referred to this committee, and that our findings are acted upon. This particular matter has implications outside the particular department concerned, so there is every reason why we should have discussed it.

Management representatives. This matter concerned only one department, so there was no need for it to be referred to this committee. If every matter of this kind were referred to this committee, the delays would be endless. Also, we must get it understood that this committee is only advisory.

Personnel manager. This committee could do a lot of good in improving communications, but we must keep off dangerous matters like whether or not it is only advisory. It is best to let 'understandings' evolve. Also, I am not satisfied that the workers' representatives are in fact in close communication with the workers. I think they are keeping things to themselves, and see themselves as becoming a new source of power similar to the shop stewards. This would defeat the whole object of the exercise.

Case 6 The new machine

Characters: Works Manager
Union Convenor

Background to the case

At present the product is made on two machines, each operated by two skilled workmen. A new machine has become available which will produce a greater quantity than the two existing machines together, and can be operated by one semi-skilled workman.

Works Manager. We have to introduce the new machine, because whether or not we do, our rivals will, and since the cost per article will be much lower, we should be out of business. So I must get it over to the unions that the choice is between fewer jobs or no jobs at all.

Union Convener. I can see that the new machine has to come. What I must do is to get the best terms I can for the four men at present employed. I know that still leaves us in the end with fewer jobs for my union members, but what choice do I have?

Case 7 Trade-union recognition

Characters: Works manager
Shop steward
Full-time union official

Background to the case

Because of high unemployment in certain industries, the government have instituted emergency retraining schemes for the workers made redundant. Nationally, the craft union has promised recognition to the workers trained in this way.

One of the retrained workers has now applied to this firm for a job at a time when there is at least temporarily some unemployment in the area, even in his new trade. The shop steward is maintaining that the vacancy should go to one of the apprentice-trained unemployed, and not to this newly trained worker.

Describe the attitude which each of the above characters might adopt, and write a summary of the discussion which might take place.

13.5 Job satisfaction

An adult spends nearly half his waking hours at work. For most people their job is their only source of income, and their standard of living depends on it. Nevertheless, people have very different attitudes towards their work, as you will see by reading the following case studies.

1   Bill Gregory

Bill left school at fifteen and took a job as a clerk in a small manufacturing firm. After a year as a 'tea-boy' he was given some more varied and interesting work, and eventually he was helping to deal with customers' queries and complaints. But when he was twenty-one he wanted to get married. He found he wasn't saving fast enough and he didn't see much chance of promotion, so he took his present job as a machine operator – 'for the money'.

He is now thirty-six, is married, and has two children. He lives in a small private semi-detached house and he has a car. He has spent a lot of time improving the house, and he has an allotment where he grows most of his own vegetables. He goes fishing with a club on Sundays. He says he is very happily married, and his wife has a part-time job as a shop assistant which brings them in enough to go on a package holiday to Spain each year.

He makes no secret of the fact that he does the job entirely for the money. He is often bored, and he day-dreams a lot. He misses the friendly contacts which he had in his clerical job. Although he is a union member, he has never been to a branch meeting. He is not a member of the social club, and he never sees his workmates outside work. The only people he recognises as friends are in the angling club, and the only people he visits, or is visited by, are relations.

2   Jenny Wright

Jenny Wright is a social worker in her mid twenties, married to a school-teacher. She describes her salary as 'inadequate', and the hours she works as 'excessive'. She works in a large city, dealing with the old, the sick, the down-and-out, the dishonest. Her job is often depressing, and she worries about the effect that her experiences are having on her personality. Nothing shocks her any more, and her husband complains that she has become unsympathetic.

Jenny went into social work as a vocation, because she felt that she would be helping the community. She still holds this attitude to some extent, but admits that often she doesn't feel particularly useful, because the problems are so great and her efforts are so small. She enjoys the independence that she has at work, and enjoys making decisions. She sees the job as a challenge, and would not readily give it up.

3   Jack Belcher

Jack Belcher is a retired, self-employed grocer, and tells his own story.

'My shop was situated in a densely populated suburb of a large city. I became the owner of the shop in 1967, buying out my partner who retired. Even then I worked long hours – a minimum of 60 hours per week. In the early 1970's, competition from supermarkets badly affected my business. I sacked my full-time assistant and managed with two part-time assistants instead. I started to work about 75 hours per week, and had no holidays at all.

'I worked hard so that I could afford to educate my three children. I had little formal education, and I wanted my children to have a start in life which my parents could not give me. All my children have university degrees and are well-established in their careers. None works particularly long hours, and all have good salaries. Ill-health forced me to retire three years ago, but any sacrifice that I have made is worth it. My children will achieve things in life that have been denied to me, and that is all the satisfaction that I require.'

4   David Long

David Long is twenty-seven years old, and is unmarried. He is a clerk in the purchase invoice department of a large car factory. His job is to examine invoices (or bills) as they come in to the factory, check that the goods charged for have actually been received, and clear the invoices for payment. It is a routine sort of job. David says he 'doesn't mind it', but also admits that he could and should be doing something better.

His trouble, so he says cheerfully, is that he can't be bothered. He can't be bothered to get to work on time; he can't be bothered to dress smartly; he can't be bothered even to read the newspaper. He is completely unambitious, says he earns enough to live on, and declares that he would never work on the production line even though he could almost double his wages.

David enjoys life outside the factory. He watches the local football team play on Saturday afternoons. He referees football matches on Sunday mornings. He plays cribbage, darts, and dominoes expertly. He says that his wages enable him to do what he wants to do, and that he is perfectly happy.

Write a short paragraph on each of the four characters, explaining what motivates them.

Bill Gregory, in one of our case studies above, said that his job was very boring.

Bill is employed on a mass-production line. As the product (car,

Metal finishers working on a traditional car assembly line

refrigerator, etc.) moves along the line, each man does one very simple job on it – fits a wind-screen wiper, or brake light, or exhaust pipe. A relatively unskilled man soon becomes very proficient at his particular task, but also he may become very bored. Some people say that workers employed on this sort of job are more likely to go on strike just to get some variety out of life. Someone said, 'Most of us spend most of our lives doing jobs we don't really like to produce articles we don't really need.' Ought we to reorganise work so that many more people can have interesting jobs? Attempts to do this are called 'job enrichment'.

The Volvo motor-car company in Sweden has used job enrichment for some years now, especially in their plant at Kalmar. The labour force is divided up into groups of about twenty workers, and each group completes one major stage in the production process, e.g. one group might install the complete electrical system.

The factory building is simply a collection of production bays, and parts and components are moved from one bay to another by a system of electrical trolleys. Workers swap tasks regularly, discuss the organisation of the work, and can transfer from one work unit to another from time to time to do a different kind of work. Each room has its own entrance, its own changing room, its own coffee room and its own assembly area of about 1000 square metres, where the work is done; i.e., each team is given a territory that can be seen as its own small workshop within the larger plant, and this promotes team spirit. Thus workers can gain some measure of satisfaction from their work, and take a pride in the cars that they are manufacturing.

Employees work in small
groups at the Kalmar
factory

Volvo took something of a risk. In 1974 their Kalmar factory cost 10%
more to build than a conventional car factory. If anything, the production
process is probably more costly in theory than the traditional production
line. But Volvo have gained in the following ways:

1 Less absenteeism of workers.

2 Fewer industrial disputes.

3 No problems in recruiting a labour force with the appropriate skills.

4 High standards of workmanship, resulting in better cars. This has
   enabled Volvo to save money on repairs carried out under guarantee
   and has also boosted the company's reputation for making reliable
   motor cars.

It must be understood that Volvo had strictly economic motives for
introducing this new system. The company expected to produce more
cars more efficiently and more cheaply, and consequently to sell more and
to make more profit. It has succeeded.

There are other ways of coping with boring, repetitive jobs. With
extensive use of robot technology, for example, the Japanese have succeeded in eliminating many of these, especially in their motor car industries. Similarly, in 1980, when British Leyland introduced the Mini Metro
the design of the production plant relied very heavily on the use of robot
arms.

Both robot technology and job enrichment cut out semi-skilled jobs.

Discuss with your teacher:

1   How important is job satisfaction to employees?
2   What effects do you think an increase in methods of either job enrichment or robot technology will have on job opportunities in the future?

Robot arms at work
on a Metro
body shell

Document 13A Membership of some unions, 1980

Name of Union	Number of members	Name of Union	Number of members
Transport and General Workers Union	2 086 281	National Union of Mineworkers	253 142
Amalgamated Union of Engineering Workers	1 217 760	National Society of Metal Mechanics	50 369
General and Municipal Workers Union	967 153	Prison Officers Association	20 469
National Union of Teachers	248 896	Military and Orchestral Musical Instrument Makers Trade Society	226
		Wool Shear Workers Trade Union	30

Document 13B The background to two industrial disputes

1 Dock workers

The employers in the docks are trying to introduce machinery to handle the new container traffic. At the same time they wish to reduce the labour force in order to keep costs and prices steady. The dockers are striking to get better redundancy agreements – fewer dockers made redundant, and more compensation for those who have to go.

All the dockers are members of the same union. About a quarter of all the goods we consume come in from abroad, and about a quarter of what we produce is exported. Without the dockers, imports and exports would virtually cease. In an emergency the government could use troops to handle cargoes, but there is a possibility that this would lead to violence.

2 Post Office workers

Many Post Office workers are poorly paid, and they are striking for a particularly large pay increase. The strike is official, but the union does not have sufficient funds to give strike pay. They had hoped for financial support from other unions, but this has not been forthcoming.

Document 13C Working days lost through stoppages

1 Stoppages in years 1974–79

Total number of working days lost through stoppages

Year	(Thousands)
1974	14 750
1975	6 012
1976	3 284
1977	10 142
1978	9 405
1979	29 474

2 International comparison of days lost through industrial disputes: days lost per 1000 employees

	Average 1963–7	1975
France	325	177
W. Germany	54	21
Italy	1 481	222
Japan	213	87
Sweden	44	3
Switzerland	6	0.7
United Kingdom	576	282
United States	1 232	297

14 Making bigger profits

The directors of a firm have many aims, but one of these is certainly to make bigger profits. Sometimes this is because they wish to use the profits as capital to expand the firm, and sometimes it is to distribute them to the shareholders.

We are going to look at the ways in which, as directors of a firm, we might try to make larger profits, and then in Section 15 we are going to ask whether the consumer needs to be protected against any of the actions we might be tempted to take.

"Well this is the space-saving car of the future, but how are we going to get people that small?"

14.1 Value analysis

One way of increasing our profits would be to manufacture our product more cheaply. In industry, this process is sometimes called 'value analysis'. We examine our product and ask ourselves the following questions:

1 Are we making the product better than the customer really wants? For example, if we are manufacturing a pen-knife with a lot of 'gadgets', does the customer use all the gadgets? If not, we can make it cheaper by leaving off the ones which are never used. Another example: if we are manufacturing paper plates, it is no use giving them a surface finish which will stand up to wiping, because they are thrown away after use.

2 Can cheaper material be used for any part of the product?

3 Can any components be replaced by cheaper standard components? (Examine record-players in shops: you will find that most makes use the same record-changing mechanism.)

4 Would a minor change in design eliminate or reduce wastage of material during manufacture, or eliminate any manufacturing process? For example, a certain cooker used to be manufactured by welding metal sheets together; now a large section of it is stamped out of one sheet of metal, thus eliminating some very time-consuming welding.

5 Are all the surface finishes essential?

Example 1

A shoe manufacturer carried out a value analysis on a pair of women's holiday shoes, with the following results:

		Saving
a)	Shoe upper and insole: used less expensive material which passed the same wear test.	3·78%
b)	Heel piece: material used to reinforce heel piece was different from that used for the insole; the new material was used for both.	0·63%
c)	Lace: round lace used instead of flat lace.	0·80%
d)	Eyelets: consequent reduction in size of eyelet.	0·46%
e)	Outsole: change in process of moulding and cutting to give less wastage.	9·85%
	Total	15·52%

Example 2

1 At one time, stools in school laboratories were made entirely out of wood. Modern stools have a metal frame and a plastic seat. Describe the process of value analysis which led to this change. What effect would the change have in the factory where the stools are manufactured?

2 Carry out a value analysis on a typical wooden sideboard.

3 Carry out a value analysis on your own product.

4 In what way might a manufacturer abuse this process of value analysis?

14.2 Expansion of sales

Another method of increasing profits is to expand our sales. How can we expand? The obvious ways are (a) by selling more of the same product, (b) by starting to manufacture a similar product which uses the same raw materials (so that we can buy in bulk) and employs similar manufacturing processes (so that we can make economies in our production line).

Suppose we decide to manufacture more of the same product. If there is a good sale for it, we had better expand to satisfy the home market quickly, or some other manufacturer will cut in. So we invest heavily in machinery and set up a mass-production line. But suppose our product is durable or semi-durable, such as electric fires or carpets (as distinct from consumables such as bread or washing-up liquid); what happens when nearly every household has one, so that the market is saturated?

We have had to invest heavily to set up a mass-production line in order to prevent anyone else cutting in on our market, but, when the market is saturated, we have all that investment left on our hands.

There are several methods which we might use to help us out of this dilemma.

1 Persuading people to buy more than one of our product

For example, suppose we manufacture carpets, and families are used to buying a square of carpet for the centre of their main room. We could

Do you need a second set?

persuade them that they need wall-to-wall carpet, and that they need it in every room of the house.

2 Making our durable a little less durable

A trade journal reported some time ago that some manufacturers of refrigerators were not using the most durable plastics available at the price. The one used was likely to discolour and crack after a period of normal home use.

Rust marks on the wing of a car

89

The interior of a transistor radio

3 Making our product difficult to repair

If our product includes an electric light bulb, we could make the part which contains the bulb as a sealed unit so that, if the bulb blew, the whole unit would have to be replaced. By pricing the replacement unit at only slightly less than the complete product, most people would be persuaded to have a new product rather than have it repaired.

4 'Improving' our product

Suppose we manufacture hand-push lawn-mowing machines. We might change to manufacturing power mowers, and persuade people they need these instead of their hand mowers. Since gardens are getting smaller and most men say they do not get enough exercise, this might prove a little difficult, but we could try it. Alternatively, we might introduce 'friction-less' bearings on our hand machines. The 'improvement' need not be of great importance.

5   Making fashion changes

Suppose we manufacture lamp shades. We could ring the changes on colours – 'this year's colour is pastel blue' – or style and ornamentation – very plain one year, very ornamental the next. Of all the methods for expanding our sales, fashion changes probably offer the most scope.

A boutique window – full of the latest fashions

1   Imagine you manufacture each of the following products. Devise ways in which you might develop your product.
   a) Tights
   b) Swimsuits
   c) Wrist-watches
   d) Do-it-yourself tools
   Then do the same for the product your class chose to manufacture.

2   Can you think of actual cases, not necessarily with these products, where you think these methods have been applied? Read Documents 14A and 14B.

3 As a customer, how do you feel about the practices we have thought about? Find out whether there are any ways in which the customer is protected against these practices.

4 If these practices were pursued to any great extent, what problems might be raised by (a) the exhaustion of our natural resources, (b) the disposal of industrial and household waste?

14.3 Advertising

If we wish to expand the sales of our product (or, indeed, to sell our product in any quantity) we must be prepared to advertise it.

Advertising has two functions:

1 to provide information about the product,

2 to persuade people to buy the product.

We have seen in the previous section that a mass-production firm must keep demand for its product at a constant high level in order to justify the large sum of money spent on machinery.

Let us look at the case of a manufacturer of domestic heating appliances (electric fires, gas fires, etc.). He is faced with rising and falling demand depending on the season. This seasonal fluctuation of demand is super-imposed on a gradually falling demand for gas and electric fires as more people fit central heating.

As the manufacturer, I might analyse the situation as follows.

What are the limitations of central heating?

1 It may be relatively slow in warming up a room from cold.

2 It may be slow to adapt room temperature to rapidly changing out-door temperatures, so that there are several months during the spring and autumn when it can cause discomfort by keeping a room too cold or by making it too warm.

3 It may be relatively uneconomic to run under the above conditions.

Therefore as manufacturers we must develop our fire so that it will:

a) give out a lot of heat quickly when needed,

b) turn down to a relatively low level of heat production when necessary.

If we do this, then we may have a strong argument for persuading customers to fit a fire as well as central heating. If we emphasise the spring and autumn use we can stimulate demand at times when it would otherwise be slack.

Having developed our product in the way we think it will be most useful to the public, we must now put our arguments over in such a way that they will buy – we must advertise. At this stage we should probably hire a specialist firm to organise the advertising of our product. This type of firm is called an advertising agency, and the agency will provide us with an advertising campaign suitable for our product.

The important media which carry advertising are television, newspapers, and magazines. A thirty-second item on television costs about the same as a full-page display in a national newspaper, i.e. a half-page or quarter-page display is cheaper than a spot on television. Television is appropriate if we are aiming at all sections of the public, or the majority of the public, but if we are aiming at a particular section then it might be cheaper and just as effective to use one or more of the national newspapers, which are more selective in their readership.

1 Obtain copies of all the national newspapers and decide which of the occupational groups A, B, C1, C2, D, and E are most likely to read each paper (see Table 2A).

2 Which categories are most likely to buy fires in the way we plan?

3 Would you use television or one or more newspapers? If newspapers, which would you use?

4 List other ways by which a manufacturer might advertise his product. Would these methods be suitable for advertising gas or electric fires?

Having decided where to advertise, we must decide on the form of our advertising. We have decided to emphasise that our fire will warm a room quickly, and that in the spring and autumn it is more economic to use a gas or electric fire than central heating, because it can easily be controlled to adapt to varying external temperatures. Now we must do market research to find out whether these arguments will convince the public, and how we can put them across so that they will be convincing. We must also try to find out whether there are any other qualities the public requires in a domestic fire, and if necessary we must adapt our product to incorporate them.

Equally important, we must find out whether the public has any resistances to the purchase of fires. For example, if we manufacture gas fires, we might find that people think gas fires are undesirable because they use up all the air in a room, or because they give off harmful fumes. The difficulty in this kind of market research is that people may not be consciously aware of their prejudices. Advertising agencies often employ psychologists to investigate customers' motives (motivational research), and some of these try to discover unconscious resistances by using word-association tests – the psychologist says a word, and the customer says the first word which comes into his mind. For example, a test might run: apple . . . orange; fork . . . knife; gas fire . . . fumes. If there are any resistances of this kind, then we must frame our advertising to overcome them.

Having drawn up our advertisement, we must check that the public understands it, and that it has no unconscious implications of a detrimental nature. For example, one brewer decided to advertise a brand of beer as low-calorie – less fattening. But on investigation it was found that this implied to the average customer that his other beers were very fattening, and that the low-calorie brand had been in some way denatured, so that it would be less satisfying. None of these implications was much help to the brewer, so the campaign was dropped.

Obviously we must direct our advertising so that not only does the customer go to the gas-board showroom to buy a fire, but when he gets there he buys *our* fire and not that of one of our competitors. So, having found out what the customer desires most in a gas fire, we must create the impression that our fire has it, and by implication the others do not. This is called creating the 'brand image'. For example, our jingle might be, 'Northern – the spring and autumn fire – and for the British summer too!'

To make sure of our effect, we should have literature which emphasises the important features from our advertising on display at the point of sale in the showroom.

Since we are hoping to sell fires in addition to central heating, we might advertise in the trade magazine for heating engineers, suggesting that they might push our product in return for a suitable commission on sales. It is important to co-ordinate all aspects of the marketing operation.

Advertisements appeal in a variety of ways

5 Give examples of 'images' for (a) perfume, (b) cars.

6 Give examples of products which you have resisted buying because you did not like the way they were advertised.

Now let us analyse the way in which advertisers use television and the newspapers at present, to discover whether the ideas we have formulated are in fact practised.

We will analyse the television commercials for a particular evening under the following headings.

A   What is the duration of the commercial in seconds?

B   Does the commercial give information about the product, or reasons for using the product, which seems reasonably reliable?

C   Does the commercial make claims for the product which would be impossible to prove, or difficult to prove, or are meaningless?

D   Does the commercial make claims which seem grossly exaggerated?

E   Is the commercial designed to overcome resistances?

F   Is the commercial designed to create a brand image?

G   Does it use a jingle to do this (e.g. 'For mash get Smash')?

H   Does the commercial seek to create, by implication, a mood of enjoyment (for example, implying that if you smoke our cigars you will feel happy all the time, or if you use our hair-spray you will feel radiant and attractive)?

You will probably be surprised to find that each evening between five o'clock and eleven o'clock there are about 100 commercials each lasting from 10 to 30 seconds, so our exercise will require careful organising. It is suggested that you each make out a table like this:

Time	Name of product	A	B	C	D	E	F	G	H
17.00	Peanut Treets	20					√	√	√
	Teflon saucepans	15	√				√		
	PG Tips (tea)	20					√	√	√

You will then need to operate in teams. Each person fills in the time and the name of the product (which often comes towards the end of the commercial), and scrutinises the commercial for one of the aspects A, B, C, ... which are ticked where appropriate as in the examples.

In the following lesson, each team can amalgamate its results. Items C, D, E, and H will probably require discussion.

7 How far is our idea that television commercials will be used mainly for products which are bought in quantity by most sections of the public borne out by your analysis?

8 Do you think that advertisers choose the time of showing according to the section of the public they wish to reach?

9 Are there more commercials at some times during the evening? Since there is a rule that commercials can be shown only at 'natural breaks' in the programme, does this seem to influence the form of the programmes?

10 Are there any commercials which are shown more than once during the evening? Are there any products which are advertised by two or more different commercials?

11 Is there any kind of trade 'war' going on (for example, two soap manufacturers each taking a large share of the commercials)?

Now let us analyse the newspaper advertising. Obtain copies of the principal national dailies, and also of the local daily if there is one. Note the price of each, and find out the circulation. For each newspaper, measure the total area of newsprint and the area devoted to advertising. Look through the newspapers and classify the types of advertisement – you might decide on the following classifications.

A   Products, e.g. cigarettes.
B   Services, e.g. airlines, car hire.
C   Entertainment.
D   Investment.
E   Property for sale.
F   Jobs vacant.

Measure the area devoted to each. Then complete the following table:

Name of newspaper	Price	Circula-tion	Area of newsprint	Area of adverts	% adverts	A	B	C	D	E	F
Times											
Guardian											
Daily Telegraph											
Daily Express											
Daily Mail											
Sun											
Daily Mirror											
Daily Star											
Local daily											

For each newspaper, list the products advertised in panels of area greater than 16 cm^2.

12 Is there any marked difference between the percentage area devoted to advertising in each paper? Is there any relationship between this and the price and circulation?

13 Is there any marked difference between the types of advertising in each paper? If so, why do you think this is?

14 Are the products and services advertised in the newspapers markedly different in any way from those advertised on television?

15 Do the products and services advertised vary in any way from one newspaper to another? If so, does it bear out our idea that different newspapers are aimed at different sections of the public?

16 Do you think people would be prepared to pay more for newspapers and magazines which contained no advertising?

We have now looked at advertising in some detail and seen how it fits into the overall concept of 'marketing'. The following questions are concerned with some other aspects of marketing.

17 Suppose you are given the job of marketing a liquid detergent which you know to be more or less the same as those made by other manufacturers. Describe how you would go about it so that you would gain the largest share of the market.

18 Go to your local supermarket, make a list of all the detergents and soaps, and look on the packet or wrapper for the name of the manufacturer of each one. You will find that each manufacturer makes several detergents and soaps. Why do you think this is?

19 Suppose we had created a successful 'brand image' for a brand of clothing, and we were approached by a chain store who asked us to sell them the same article which they would then retail under their own brand name, but cheaper than the price at which we were selling it. Would you agree? Why might they be able to sell it without our brand advertising?

20 It has been discovered by market research that very few customers in supermarkets go in with a shopping list: they shop on impulse.
   Suppose we decide to market fresh fruit juice, and part of our campaign will be to promote impulse buying in supermarkets. Formulate the marketing campaign you would mount, giving reasons for all your decisions.

21 In what ways do you think the use of advertising could be abused? Read Document 14C.

22 Suppose we lived in a planned economy, where a central organisation decided what products should be manufactured, how much of each, and the prices at which they should be sold. Would market research and advertising have any uses? Might they be different in any way?

23 When we were thinking about the marketing of the liquid detergent which was very little different from our rivals' products, we tried to find out what the public wanted, and to imply in our advertising that our product had these qualities but our rivals' products did not. Could the same techniques be applied to promoting a political party or a political leader at an election? Do you think there is any evidence that these techniques have been so applied? If they have, do you think this is in any way harmful?

24 Are there any current advertisements which try to persuade people to save money or give it to charities rather than spend it on consumer goods? Which of these do you think are the most persuasive, and why?

Now formulate an advertising campaign for your own product.

Document 14A   *The 30000 mile shock absorbers*

(From *The Sunday Times*. Prices as at 1981)

Shock absorbers are among the most vital parts of a car – affecting its safety, roadholding and general reliability as well as comfort. But they are well hidden and few people ever check whether they are in working order. Currently, however, shock absorber manufacturers are campaigning through television, posters and leaflets to make people aware that absorbers are often badly worn after 30000 miles. 'Worn shock absorbers are dangerous', says the publicity.

It seems rather extraordinary that manufacturers should publicise the speed with which their product can wear out. There is, however, as we shall see, a strong commercial motive. But even if the campaign is to the advantage of the motorist as well as to the manufacturers, there is one aspect of the situation which is omitted in the publicity: it is technically possible to mass-produce shock absorbers that would last for 100000 miles.

The ordinary shock absorber is about a foot long and usually looks something like a bicycle pump with a ring at both ends. There are four on most cars and their job is to damp down the vibration that starts when the car hits a bump or dip in the road. In the trade they are known as 'shocks' or 'shockers'.

Why it is essential to get rid of worn shockers was demonstrated graphically on August 22, 1969. On that day SAMA (the Shock Absorber Manufacturers Association) took six three-year-old cars to the Motor Industry Research Association testing circuit near Nuneaton. There were two Ford Cortinas, two Vauxhall Vivas and two Hillman Minxes. One of each pair of cars was left with its original shock absorbers, and marked, in recognition of this fact, with a skull and crossbones. The other cars were fitted with new ones. Two days earlier, all six cars had successfully negotiated MoT vehicle tests.

For five hours, never travelling at more than 40 m.p.h., the cars went round the circuit, which is specially designed to give in this time the kind of battering a car would receive from 10000 miles of everyday driving on normal roads. By the end of the day, one of the Hillmans was virtually uncontrollable on corners, one of the Fords had a broken half-shaft, and one of the Vauxhalls had parted company with its exhaust pipe. All three cars that went wrong carried the skull and crossbones: the cars with the new shock absorbers came through unscathed.

SAMA had certainly proved its point. Three officers from the Hendon Police Driving School who had come along to watch said they would have booked the three bad cars for being in a dangerous condition.

Significantly, SAMA's demonstration of how troublesome its members' products can be after three years coincided with a drive by the manufacturers to sell shock absorbers as replacements and not just as original equipment for new cars.

One shock absorber manufacturer explained to us in terms of the small family saloon why this should be economically attractive. The manufacturing cost for each shocker – most cars have four – is £7·00. The car manufacturer, after lengthy bargaining, agrees to pay £8·00 each. But in the replacement market the mark-up is very much greater: the selling price to a distributor is often as high as £11·00. And by the time it reaches the motorist, its price tag will be reading at least £21·00.

The fact that not only the makers of shockers, but the garages which sell them, can do well out of the spares market is stressed in SAMA's promotional material for garages: 'Sell shocks on your accessory counter and catch the DIY motorist as well. It's bouncing business! A new pair of shocks can make more profit than a pair of spotlamps or a pair of tyres or a new battery.'

Nowhere has the effect of selling replacement shock absorbers shown up more clearly on a company's balance sheet than in the case of Armstrong Equipment, one of Britain's largest manufacturers of shockers. Until the mid-1960s, Armstrong almost totally ignored the replacement market. Its profits drifted around the £300000 to £400000 level, dipping in 1966 to £121544. Then Armstrong began to put more emphasis on the replacement market. Profits started to rise dramatically. By 1969 they had topped the £1 million mark, and two-fifths of all sales were to the replacement market.

It follows that if the SAMA campaign succeeds, and we all get into the habit of checking regularly whether our shockers need replacing (SAMA have recently brought out a machine to make the check), many more will be sold. There will be fewer dangerous cars on the road and the directors of Armstrong, and the other companies, will find their profits soaring as a result.

But it would be perfectly possible to fit longer-lasting shock absorbers in the first place. Armstrong told us it could make them for mass production cars if the car manufacturers wanted them.

A Dutch firm called Koni already makes shockers, which it claims should normally last over 100000 miles, to fit most car models; but except for very expensive cars they are not fitted as original equipment.

Koni and Armstrong agree that to fit long-lasting shockers would add around £150 to the price of a new car – including a far higher profit margin than the car manufacturers allow them. At the moment it costs upwards of £100, including labour charges, for a complete set of new ordinary shockers to be fitted in place of a worn set. If every car had two new sets of shockers during its life, the cost would be £200–£300 more over the whole period. So there would be a financial saving to the motorist if long-lasting shockers were fitted in the first place. And added to this we have the evidence of the experiment at the MIRA circuit and the testimony of the Hendon police officers that worn shock absorbers are dangerous.

The shock absorber makers argue that they are not responsible for this situation since they supply to the specification of car manufacturers who in turn have a natural interest in cutting costs. Indeed, until recently SAMA did not really know how well or badly its members' products performed. As one Armstrong official told us: 'The trouble is that no real research has ever been done. Because shock absorber manufacturers have in the past simply supplied what the car makers wanted, we never had any reason to do research. But now the replacement market is hotting up, we are beginning to examine how long our shock absorbers last.'

Enough is now known to suggest it would be quite feasible for car manufacturers to offer long-lasting shockers, at least as an optional extra on new cars. But according to the Armstrong official, resistance to change may depend on more than the present lack of customer demand. Of the reasons for the present state of affairs, he said: 'Partly it's because of the way our economy works. It needs people to spend money consistently to keep it going. Certainly it may be cheaper in the long run to produce cars with longer-lasting components. But, you know, it may not do the economy much good.'

Document 14B   *No heat, and not very much light*

(Editorial reprinted from *The Guardian*, 4th February 1978)

At this stage of the select committee's proceedings it is not easy to know whether they are grappling with a serious burden on the householder and taxpayer or whether the durability of light bulbs, though of passing interest and conversational value, is a trifling matter to occupy so much investigative time. The allegations before the House of Commons Select Committee on Science and Technology are that manufacturers produce bulbs designed to last for 1000 hours when for little extra cost they could produce bulbs lasting twice as long, and also that the 1000-hour bulbs may last as little as 400 hours in any case. In rebuttal the manufacturers have said that there is little public demand for the long-life bulbs they do make, that they give less light, and that consequently they are more energy-intensive.

At this week's hearing the names of the Monopolies Commission, the Office of Fair Trading, and several departments of state were invoked in pursuit of the facts, and the committee adjourned dissatisfied that it had yet heard enough independent technical evidence. If there were a scandal here how great would be its proportions? If a bulb cost 20p, if it lasts its rated 1000 hours, and if it is used for eight hours a day it costs ·16p a day, or just over a penny a week, to have the light on. During its 125 weeks it will use (assuming a 100-watt bulb), electricity costing £2.54, so that the cost of the electricity is 12·5 times that of the bulb. The makers say that a 2000-hour bulb would cost 20 per cent more and give 20 per cent less light. For the same amplitude of light the consumer would thus be paying – ·12p a day instead of ·16p. After 25 days he would be a penny better off.

Given the huge turnover in bulbs there must clearly be advantages to the makers in only fractional increases in selling price or fractional falls in durability. It is these differences that appear to have aroused the suspicions. One of the departments of state not invoked at this week's hearing was the Department of Employment. What would be the effect on jobs if the makers more actively promoted the 2000-hour bulb and consumers decided to buy it? How would any resulting unemployment relate to the small fractions of a penny a day which householders would save on a lamp? This is perhaps a part of the equation which manufacturers would find embarrassing to discuss, because to accept the premises would imply that they are not serving the consumer with maximum efficiency. But it is worth looking into before the committee reports. Millions of fractional pennies might swell profits: they might equally swell dole queues.

Document 14C *Cigarette Packs: dressed to kill*

(Article from *Design*, March 1981)

'There is one product which will kill at least one in four of its users and lose the rest at least ten years of their lives. Yet it's dressed up in highly decorative, attractive packs. Its manufacturers spend hundreds of thousands of pounds in design research so more people will buy more of it. They spend more money on taking deliberate steps to try and play down the dangers to health and play up the social acceptability of smoking. It's criminal.' So David Simpson, spokesman for ASH, Britain's main anti-smoking lobby, says. Gerry Murray, who runs the packaging side of Wills, one of the UK's biggest cigarette companies sees the matter differently 'Cigarettes are a very sophisticated market. Consumers pay a lot and expect a good deal. A pack must be something they feel totally comfortable with, day in and day out.'

In a world of ironies, cigarettes represent one of the worst tangles. It's big business, successful even in times of depression, employing thousands of people in the UK. Government collect a lot of tax cash annually from the sale of billions of tiny white tubes – 51 pence from every 70 pence pack sold in Britain goes to the Treasury. Meanwhile, back in the hospital wards, the same government has to patch up the tar-scarred bodies of smoking casualties.

Smoking is undoubtedly unpleasant, dirty and dangerous, but the tradition of cigarette pack design and manufacture is a long and pleasing one. Few other packages receive the degree of loyalty, fondness (or, for that matter, fondling) that cigarette packs get. Historically, different packs have offered different overtones – gangster cool, daring female, city sophisticate, tweedy solidity, cowboy or executive-slick. Even today film stars smoke on the screen, lovers smoke in bed, and soldiers in the trenches, and, in the past at least, all of them knew every inch of their cigarette pack intimately, traced fingers over its embossed shapes, wrote 'phone numbers on it and regarded it as a constant companion.

Chris Mullen's *Cigarette pack art* (Hamlyn, 1979) excellently describes the massive, meticulous effort that has gone into devising packs. In its essential, he says, the decorated pack came into vogue after machine-made cigarettes arrived in the late nineteenth century. From the 'fifties onwards, however, there was a retreat from decoration and figurative imagery, the marketing people became nervous of alienating potential smokers and so went for minimalist stripes and other 'democratic', inoffensive mass design styles. In Britain the trend has lately been to the 'classy but classless' pack, typified by Benson & Hedges (the market leader), Lambert and Butler and John Player, and reminiscent of the first cigarette cases. Sometimes called the 'decorator pack', they're made of glossy, single colour card and look smart and strong.

While cheap cigarettes and American cigarettes still come in the one piece soft paper cup (which dominates the US market and takes about half the European), in Britain the 'crushproof' hinged lid pack, invented by design award-winning South London firm Molins after the Second World War, rules. The US top selling brand, Marlboro, was originally introduced to the UK in a soft cup, but it didn't do too well, and was pretty rapidly transferred to the hinged lid pack. Between the soft cup and the 'crushproof' came the 'hull and slide', an open container within an open-ended casing, like a box of matches. In its time, hull and slide has been used for expensive cigarettes, but now has pretty downmarket overtones – Players used it for cheap brand Weights, for example – and has become fairly rare.

Wills reckons that each empty cigarette pack costs the smoker just under one pence, less than one per cent of the retail price of the average pack of cigarettes, but about five per cent of the retail price excluding tax. The firm buys in between 13 to 14 000 tonnes of paper and board a year, which, at £5m, is worth about a tenth of the UK carton production industry's annual output, so if non-smokers have their way, it will be more than the cigarette-makers who hit hard times – carton manufacturers like Mardon Son & Hall and DRG Cartons of Bristol, Tillotson's of Liverpool, Pembroke Packaging of London and David S. Smith of Neath (as well as Molins) will also feel the pinch.

At the moment, however, things haven't come to that. Though the British Medical Association maintains that stopping smoking is probably the single most effective thing that could be done to reduce illness and death in this country, and the Government claims to want to see less people – and certainly less children – smoking, the authorities won't readily pass laws to stop advertising encouraging the practice. Instead, the Government favours voluntary agreements with the tobacco industry so that advertising can be restricted and the dangers of smoking be pointed out on every pack. Unsurprisingly the tobacco industry hasn't voluntarily agreed to very much, and there are now signs that the politicians are finally admitting that one of the most profitable and competitive industries in the world is going to have to be restrained by law if it's going to be restrained at all. Even the anti-smokers, though, don't want cigarettes banned. Simpson points out that the USA's attempt to prohibit alcohol only led to black marketeering and crime.

At the end of last year, a new voluntary code was agreed between the British Government and manufacturers. From now on there should be 30 per cent less poster advertising and no posters placed near schools or playgrounds: fewer promotional offers, and new health warnings printed on cigarettes packs. The Government had wanted more, but the manufacturers dug their heels in – an action they may regret since the agreement, which they had wanted to last for four years, is in fact only going to last for two, specifically to give the Tories time to bring in legislation before the next election in 1984.

The case of the health warning, which must be printed on all packs, posters and press advertisements, is typical. The manufacturers fought over the wording and its size and position on the pack. For the past three years there has been just one health warning, half-drowned by its preamble ('HM Government Health Department Warning: Cigarettes can seriously damage your health'). It's become a graphic cliche. The obvious solution: change the wording and put it on the pack where it will have the greatest impact. The obvious manufacturer reaction: no way.

The compromise has been the devising of new slogans both coy and bland ('Smoking may cost you more than money', 'Think first – most doctors don't smoke' or 'Think about the health risks before smoking', to take a selection). From this spring, a different slogan from the new selection must be on one third of the packs of every brand at any one time. On press and poster advertisements the warning will take up nine per cent of space instead of the present six per cent. It's only a matter of time, though, before the cigarette buying public becomes immune to the new, larger messages – if, indeed, they have much impact to start off with.

The Swedish attempt to solve this problem is to have a much larger selection of slogans (16 in all) to play with, and to require that warning information is printed on both back and front of the pack. The messages aren't vague: they're statistical/medical in content – the exact added risk of smoking to a woman taking the birth control pill or to a worker who deals with asbestos, for example.

ASH feels this is the best method for Britain too. If cigarettes have to be packaged at all, it would like to see them in the dreariest boxes imaginable, with nothing but frightening information and the manufacturer's name clearly visible. The idea is to eliminate every trace of the pride of ownership cigarette buyers have for their packs. It foreshadows, in fact, the demise of an era of packaging.

Consumer protection 15

In Section 14 we began to understand how manufacturers, for reasons which seemed perfectly proper from their point of view, might take actions which look very different from the point of view of the person who buys their products in the shops – the consumer.

We saw that action needs to be taken to ensure that:

a) the consumer is not deliberately deceived by advertising,
b) The goods which the consumer buys are of a reasonable standard, and that he is able to get satisfaction from the shopkeeper if they are not,
c) the consumer is aware of all the choices open to him, so that he does not buy one product when a cheaper or better article is available elsewhere.

The Act of Parliament called the Fair Trading Act, 1973, created a new office, that of the Director General of Fair Trading. The Director General's job is to keep under review the marketing practices which firms are employing to ensure that the interests of consumers are protected. The office may carry out investigations and suggest new legislation, and it will need to see that existing laws are being properly enforced.

Most of the laws concerned with consumer protection are enforced by the local Departments of Trading Standards and Consumer Protection (which were formerly the Weights and Measures Departments).

15.1 Advertising must not deceive

The Trades Descriptions Act, 1968, was passed in order to make various practices illegal. For example:

a) If a trader makes an untrue statement, either in writing or orally, about an article or service he is selling, then he can be fined and/or put in prison. For example, if a coat is described as 'waterproof', it must be waterproof and not showerproof. A car dealer must tell you whether the mileage on the clock is correct, to the best of his knowledge.
b) A trader must not claim that he has lowered the price of a product unless he has actually charged the old price for at least 28 days in the preceding 6 months.

This law was reinforced by the Unsolicited Goods and Services Act, 1971. It had been the practice of some firms for example to select names from a telephone directory and, without receiving an order, send books or other goods for which they then demanded payment. This act made practices of this kind illegal.

1   Make a note of any advertisements which you think are deceptive.

2   Refer back to Section 14, Question 17. Do either of the laws mentioned above stop practices such as this?

3   Some advertisements on T.V. seem to imply that if you use particular brands of certain products (cigars, deodorant etc.) you will be devastatingly attractive to the opposite sex. Does this get round the Trades Descriptions Act?

4   You may have seen advertisements which say: 'Manufacturers Recommended Price (M.R.P.) £150, Our Price £100.' Is this deceptive? Should it be made illegal?

15.2 Goods must be up to standard

For as long as people have bought and sold goods the law has required standard measures of length, weight and capacity so that consumers are not cheated by receiving less than they expect. Some of our standard measures were the yard, the pound and the gallon, but we are now 'going metric' and we are increasingly using the metre, the kilogram and the litre.

A Trading Standards Inspector at work

Inspectors from the Trading Standards Departments check the accuracy of weighing and measuring devices, for example, scales in shops, spirit measures in pubs, petrol pumps.

The weight of pre-packed food must be clearly stated on the package, and this must be in 'net' terms – the weight of the contents, not the weight of the contents plus packaging.

But 'up to standard' is not only a matter of weights and measures, it is also a matter of quality.

For long a number of independent organisations have kept a check on some types of goods. One of these organisations is the British Standards Institution. The B.S.I. tests products, and if they are up to the standard of quality, safety and suitability set by the B.S.I., they are awarded the 'kitemark'.

The Kitemark

The BEAB mark

The product will also be tested regularly after this award has been given to ensure that the manufacturer is maintaining the standard. Examples of goods that have standards laid down by law are crash helmets, car safety seats for children, and paraffin heaters.

The British Electrotechnical Approvals Board for Household Equipment (BEAB) is another organisation which deals particularly with the electrical safety of household goods, basing its tests on British Standards.

The Sale of Goods Act, 1893, reinforced by the Supply of Goods (Implied Terms) Act, 1973, entitle the buyer of an article to compensation from the seller for one or more of the following reasons:

a) if the article does not correspond to the description the seller has given; for example, if a refrigerator had a smaller cubic capacity than stated,

b) if the article is not of 'merchantable quality'; for example, if it breaks down soon after it is bought,

c) if the article is not fit for the purpose for which it was sold; for example, if a vacuum cleaner does not clean efficiently.

When action is taken under this law, the consumer deals with the retailer not the manufacturer. Even though the defect may be the fault of the manufacturer, the retailer must take the responsibility. If the customer cannot obtain satisfaction, he takes out a summons for the retailer to appear in the County Court (which is a civil court, not a criminal court). However, the lawyer's costs, even if the consumer wins the case, may be greater than the cost of the faulty article, so many people do not take action, and there are traders who take advantage of this situation. A much simpler procedure for low-cost articles has been introduced, and the Citizens' Advice Bureaux will give help to the consumers wishing to take advantage of it.

1   Make a list of the goods you see carrying the Kitemark or the BEAB mark.

2   Although goods must have on the package the net weight or volume, manufacturers may try to persuade by clever packaging. From your observations in the shops, what shapes of package and jars give an illustration of larger quantities?

3   Suppose there are three brands of toothpaste sold in a shop:

toothpaste A contains 135 cubic centimetres and costs 25p
toothpaste B contains 100 cubic centimetres and costs 20p
toothpaste C contains 125 cubic centimetres and costs 21p

Which of the three is the best value for the money?
How could this problem of comparing prices be overcome?

4   Consider again the possible abuses of value analysis and the kinds of trade practices we looked at in Section 14.2. Is the consumer effectively protected against these? Are there ways in which the consumer could be better protected?

15.3 The consumer should be aware of the choices

In 1957 the Consumers' Association was founded in this country and began to publish a monthly magazine called *Which?*.

The magazine contains detailed information about various products tested for such things as quality, cost, durability, and safety. It recommends 'good value for money' buys, and is critical of poor products. It therefore helps the consumers to decide *which* goods to choose.

The Consumers' Association also publishes specialist magazines such as *Money Which?*, *Motoring Which?*, *Handyman Which?*, and *Holiday Which?* Books are also published on certain other topics, e.g. *The Legal Side of Buying a House*, *Getting a New Job*, *Retirement*, *Stress*, *Divorce*.

Here is a list of some of the products which have been investigated by *Which?*: electronic calculators, oven cleaners, stereo cassette decks, electric irons, long-life light bulbs, fruit grading, cine projectors, tights, suitcases, toothpaste, detergents.

All the money which is needed to buy and test the products to be investigated comes from subscriptions paid by the Consumers' Association members. No money is received from industry or the government. Why

I'll wait and see what Which? says about them.

does the Consumers' Association refuse to accept money from these bodies?

No free samples for testing are accepted from manufacturers – in fact the Consumers' Association buys the goods it tests anonymously. Why do you think this should be so?

Your teacher might be able to let you see some reports from *Which?* magazines, or else your parents might be subscribers. If not, you should be able to find the magazines in the reference section of the public library.

1   Are there any other ways in which the consumer could be made better aware of the choices open to them?

15.4 Live now, Pay later

We often have the choice of buying goods or services either by paying for them immediately with cash or a cheque, or by paying for them over a period of time. A common way of paying for them over a period of time is with a bank credit card. The shop gets the money immediately from your bank, and you either settle the account with your bank at the end of the month, or pay interest on the amount you have put off paying.

Another way of spreading our payments is known as *hire purchase*. Few shops finance hire purchase themselves: they ask a finance company which specialises in hire-purchase lending to do it for them. The customer pays the shopkeeper the necessary deposit for the article, and the finance company pays the shopkeeper the rest of the money. The customer then pays his instalments, plus interest charges, to the finance company.

Why do you think that traders prefer finance companies to provide the money for hire-purchase schemes?

1　Work out the difference between the cash price and the total hire-purchase price of the goods shown above.

2　Why should goods cost more when they are bought on credit?

When goods are bought on hire purchase, they do not legally belong to the customer until the last payment has been made. Up to this time, the customer has hired the goods, and the firm to whom the instalments are being paid remains the owner, and therefore the person who is *hiring* the goods cannot sell them to somebody else until the final instalment has been paid.

3　What could the owner of the goods do if the hirer fell behind with his payments?

Hire purchase can be abused by slick door-to-door salesmen who persuade people to buy goods they cannot really afford and then take them back when the hirer falls behind with the instalments. In 1964 the government

"Nothing much . . . one of those wretched door salesmen called yesterday"

HEATH

passed a law to protect the consumer against this. The law states that when an HP agreement is signed at home, or anywhere else other than at a shop or finance-company office, then the person buying the goods (the hirer) has three days to change his mind and write cancelling his agreement. But, even so, some salesmen now try to get the housewife to an office to sign the agreement.

Another form of instalment buying is known as a *credit sale*. Financially, this method is no different from hire purchase; the difference is a legal one. When something is bought by means of a credit sale, the customer owns the goods as soon as he pays the deposit or the first instalment. If he fails to keep up the payments, the trader cannot reclaim the goods without going to a court of law.

Over £2800 million was borrowed on HP in Great Britain in 1973, and most of this was for the purchase of 'consumer durables', e.g. television sets, washing machines, cars, etc.

4 What are the advantages and disadvantages of buying goods by hire purchase or credit sale?

When goods are bought on credit, a rate of interest is charged, and this is generally high. For example, when *Money Which?* did a survey of interest rates in October 1981, it was found that, while a personal loan from a bank cost 20–23%, HP loans could vary between 23 and 60%, and were sometimes even higher! Why do you think that the HP rates of interest are so high?

The shopper should also distinguish between the 'nominal' and the 'true' rate of interest. The most important one for the shopper is the true rate of interest, and under the Consumer Credit Act, 1974, this must now be indicated to the customer.

Why should the 'nominal' rate of interest differ from the 'true' rate? The interest charge is calculated on the total amount of money which the buyer borrows and does not take into consideration the fact that, say, over a two-year agreement half the money has been repaid at the end of the first year. Interest during the second year charged is on the full amount of money borrowed, even though only half this figure has still to be repaid. Therefore over two years the true rate of interest is nearly twice the nominal rate of interest. So a consumer should always find out from the trader the true rate of interest.

The multinational company 16

Imagine you are the managing director of a firm which has developed a new synthetic fibre for the manufacture of cloth. You realise that as well as the sales in the UK there is a good market for this cloth in other countries, for example in the Far East and in Australia/New Zealand. One possibility is to export fibre and cloth, but since wage-rates are much lower in Singapore, for example, you decide to establish factories there for the production of cloth for that market.

1 What effect will your decision have on employment in the UK?

2 What effect will your decision have on the balance of payments for the UK?

3 In order to restrict demand the British government decides to increase interest rates. You therefore decide to transfer money from Singapore to Britain.
  How might your action have been contrary to the intentions of the British government?

4 Most countries wish to be bases for international firms in order to provide employment. What inducements might they offer firms?

5 Some examples of multinational companies are Esso, IBM, ITT, Colgate–Palmolive, Goodyear, Unilever. What are the main products of these firms?

6 Can you give any other examples of multinational companies and their main products?

7 The turnover of the larger multinational companies is greater than the GDP of many smaller countries. What is the significance of this for the questions above?

Part 3 Allocating our resources—the choice before us

Demand and supply 17

17.1 Characteristics of the markets in different products

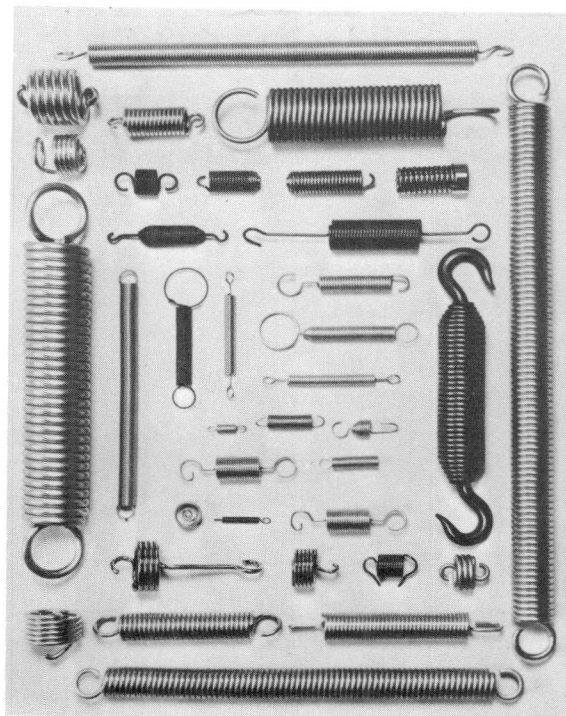

Some manufactured goods – such as ball-bearings, springs, and electric motors – are sold as components to other manufacturers, whereas others are finished products which are sold direct to the consumer, e.g. detergents, washing machines, and motor cars.

Finished products are sometimes further classified as consumables or consumer durables. Consumables are used up soon after purchase, e.g. food, drink, cigarettes, and detergents. Consumer durables are used over a period of time (but not for ever!), e.g. furniture, television sets, and cars. The distinction is not a rigid one, and items such as crockery and clothes might be classified either way.

The total amount of a particular commodity which all the customers together wish to buy *and* have the means to buy is called the 'demand'. Obviously this demand is influenced by various factors such as the price, and we shall be looking into this in more detail below.

A washing machine – a consumer durable

Packets of detergent – consumables

The total amount of a particular commodity which all the suppliers together are prepared to offer for sale is called the supply, and we shall be particularly interested in looking at how the supply of a particular commodity is adjusted to the demand.

As we saw in earlier sections, the term 'market' does not refer to any particular place, but to all the means whereby sellers and buyers come together for the purpose of making transactions.

a) The market for detergents

One factor which determines the demand for detergents (as for any other product) is customers' habits and preferences. In this case it will depend on how often they wash their clothes. Over a period of time, of course, habits may alter. As more washing machines are bought, people may wash clothes more frequently. People may be persuaded by advertising that they need to wash their clothes more frequently. Both these influences would increase the total demand for detergents.

At any particular time we would expect that if we increased or decreased the price of detergents by moderate amounts it would have little effect on the demand – people's habits would remain the same, and there is no substitute for detergents to which they could switch if the price increased. The demand for detergents is therefore said to be 'inelastic' (or, strictly, 'price-inelastic').

If we look at Table 17A we see that the manufacture of detergents is concentrated in the hands of a few firms – mainly, in fact, Lever Bros and Proctor and Gamble. One reason for this is that detergent is a fairly standardised product which is used in large quantities, and therefore the costs are lower if it is produced in large quantities.

How do manufacturers compete with each other? Those of you who have done experiments on comparing detergents will no doubt have found that all detergents are more or less the same, and it would not be a matter of great inconvenience if there were only one brand on the market.

However, it is the practice of firms to make relatively minor differences between various brands, and then try to persuade us by brand advertising that their particular product is the only one for us. This is called 'product differentiation', and seems to be the main way in which firms compete.

A little research in the grocers will show you that in terms of price per quantity there appears to be little competition between the established brands. What seems to happen is that from time to time a particular firm brings in a new 'improvement', e.g. enzymes. After initial 'introductory offers', to get it established, the new brand is more highly priced. Then other firms bring out similar products, and a common price becomes established. It is easy for this to happen because there are only a small number of firms concerned, and often one firm acts as price-leader and the others follow suit. Later these brands might suffer competition from a new 'improvement', and they might be reduced in price in order to compete.

When earlier in this section we said that the demand for detergents is probably fairly inelastic, we were speaking of the demand for detergents as a whole. The demand for a particular brand of detergent will be much more elastic, because, if it is priced very much higher than its competitors, customers will switch to another brand – unless the manufacturer can persuade us that it has such excellent qualities that it is worth the much higher price.

If there were price competition, it would be very cut-throat. If a particular firm cut its prices, it might get more trade, but because the total demand is inelastic the extra trade must come from its rivals, who would in turn cut their prices, until no-one was making a profit. This is probably why firms behave on a 'do-as-you-would-be-done-by' principle.

b) The market for margarine

The characteristics of the market for margarine are in many ways similar to those of the market for detergents; the chief difference is that margarine has a competitor in butter.

During the 1960's and early 1970's the total demand for yellow fats (margarine together with butter) remained fairly constant, but the demand for margarine fell whereas the demand for butter rose. This was during the period when standards of living in Britain were generally rising rapidly and as margarine had always had the image of a poor man's butter in this country (but not apparently in the USA) the housewives turned to butter as they became more affluent.

Since then, however, people in Britain have been made acutely aware of health hazards, particularly diseases of the heart, associated with smoking and bad eating habits. There is now strong medical evidence suggesting that too much cholesterol in the body, which is created by the consumption of saturated fatty foods, is one of the main causes of heart disease. Butter is very high in saturated fatty acids (about 60%).

The margarine manufacturers were quick to seize the opportunity and use experience gained in the USA to identify three main types of product differentiation for the sale of margarine:

1. Soft polyunsaturated, which is not only low in saturated fat (about 20%), but which some medical opinion claims actually helps to reduce the amount of cholesterol in the body. Characteristics are a pleasant taste, easy to spread, but it is relatively expensive. Its appeal is to those who are health conscious and can afford to buy it.

2. Soft with low fat saturated content (from 23%–43%). Characteristics are a pleasant taste, easy to spread, and considerably cheaper than the polyunsaturated.

3. Hard and often packaged like butter, it contains almost the same saturated fat content as butter (50%–60%). Characteristics are that it looks and tastes like butter – 'You can't tell the difference' – but it is cheaper than butter.

We would expect that the demand for margarine would be more elastic than, say, the demand for detergents because there is a close substitute in butter. Indeed the butter producers have launched a campaign to undermine some of the health claims of polyunsaturated margarine and to stress the qualities of natural dairy products. They say that butter tastes better and provided it, like most other things, is eaten in moderation, there is absolutely no health risk. It is also interesting to notice that the advice given to consumers in *Which?* (January, 1982) was: 'Take no notice of competing butter and margarine advertisements. There are no conclusive scientifically established virtues in eating one rather than the other.' So we may again reach the situation where, if the price of margarine rises significantly, more customers will switch back to butter.

Again, it should be noted, the manufacture of margarine is in the hands of a few large firms who compete by product differentiation and brand advertising rather than by charging a lower price than their competitors.

c) The market for washing machines

Washing machines are consumer durables, so we would expect the demand to be determined not only by the washing habits of customers, but by how many have been sold already. You might like to think about whether firms try to change this situation by the kind of marketing methods we discussed in Section 14.

We would expect the demand for washing machines to be fairly elastic – if the manufacturers can lower the price, it will bring washing machines within the purchasing power of less-wealthy people, and therefore they can sell more.

This being the case, we might expect that there would be price competition, though this would not be so cut-throat as with detergents for example. Experience shows, however, that competition among makes is again mainly by product differentiation and brand advertising, although there is sometimes price competition between retailers in the same area.

d) The market for beef

The characteristics of the market for beef are very different from those of the other products we have been considering.

In the first place, we would expect the demand to be very elastic, because there are close substitutes in lamb, pork, poultry, and fish.

Secondly, there are many farmers who supply beef cattle, which are sold to butchers by auction, so that the price is very sensitive to changes in demand and supply. If the demand is greater than the supply, auction prices will be high – but not too high or consumers will switch to some other meat. If the supply is greater than the demand, prices will fall – but not too low or consumers will switch from other meats. Nevertheless, there will be greater fluctuations in the price of beef than in that of, say, detergents.

1 In a manner similar to the examples above, describe what you think are the characteristics of the markets for (a) instant coffee, (b) petrol, (c) vacuum cleaners, and (d) eating apples.

17.2 Price competition

We see from Table 17A that for many products the market is dominated by a few large firms, and in the previous section we noted that these firms rarely compete directly by cutting prices, especially where the demand is inelastic. What is to prevent these firms from unofficially agreeing a price which will give them very large profits?

The basic reason is said to be competition, or fear of competition. If profits were high on product X then other firms which were not making such high profits on other products would start to make product X and sell it at a slightly lower price, and this would happen until the level of profits came down to a 'normal' level.

Thus when it was thought that Yeoman and Smash were making high profits from instant mashed potato, retailers such as Sainsbury, Tesco and Fine Fare entered the market with their own-label brands at lower prices and soon took a quarter of the market. Similarly, the Metal Box Company, who have a near-monopoly of tin cans for food and drink, told the Monopolies Commission that their profit was fixed by the difference between the cost at which they could manufacture the cans and the cost at which their large customers would be able to manufacture the cans for themselves.

1 How do firms try to maintain a higher price despite potential competition from new entrants to the market?

2 In order to start up production in competition, a firm needs more capital. What means exist for firms to obtain new capital?

3 Why will there be some delay while a firm changes from manufacturing an obsolete product to manufacturing a very different product?

4   If a government felt that there was not sufficient competition among firms in this country to keep the price of a particular product down to a reasonable level, what steps might it take?

5   If a firm were making very high profits, it would be expected to show up as a high profit as a percentage of capital employed. Figures for some large firms are given in *The Times Top 1000*. On the basis of these, is there any evidence that the large firms which dominate some industries use their position to make 'excessive' profits?

17.3 The changing pattern of demand

Consumer preferences change over a period of time, and obviously firms try to change them by advertising. Some experts have maintained that large firms can get us to buy pretty well whatever they choose to make, but read Document 17A and decide how far you think they can go in this.

An important reason for changes in demand is the invention of new products. The demand for wool and cotton declined because of the invention of synthetic fibres such as Nylon and Terylene.

Another reason is population changes. If there is an increase in the birth rate, this will show itself first in an increased demand for baby foods etc., later in a greater demand for teenage products, and finally in a greater demand for housing and household goods.

Change in real income (i.e. allowing for inflation) is another important cause of change in demand, and this will affect different products in different ways. If everyone in the country becomes more affluent, we would not expect them to buy a lot more potatoes and bread, but we would expect them to buy other types of food and more products such as washing machines and cars.

Changes in demand caused by changes in personal income will depend on the way in which the additional income is distributed. If it goes to those who have relatively low incomes it will probably increase the demand for mass-produced non-essential goods such as the cheaper radios, tape-recorders, etc. If it goes to those who already have high incomes, it will alter the demand for a different range of products.

The demand for some products affects the demand for others in a complementary way; thus an increase in the number of cars will increase the demand for petrol. These products are sometimes said to be in joint demand.

1   Look at Table 17B. What are the main items for which demand has fallen? What explanation can you offer?

2   What are the main items for which demand has risen? What explanation can you offer?

3   What changes in demand will result if the birth rate in Britain continues to fall? In the short term? In the long term?

17.4 How the market responds to the changing pattern of demand

There are a variety of different situations which can arise because of the changing pattern of demand. We shall look at two or three of these.

a) The supply may be greater than a falling demand, so that firms are not able to sell all their production.

In the long run, some of the firms must close down, and the capital and labour be moved to other industries, but this is obviously a situation which is resisted by all concerned: the shareholder and managers will lose money, and the workers will lose their jobs. The workers may be unable to find other jobs in the same trade in the same part of the country, or in any other part of the country. Unemployment which results from this cause is sometimes called 'structural' unemployment. There may be jobs in the same trade in other parts of the country, but there is the difficulty and expense of moving to consider. Those who own houses will have difficulty in selling in an area which has increasing unemployment, and those in council houses are in an even worse position. We referred to this problem of 'geographical' unemployment in Section 11.2; we shall be looking at other causes of unemployment in Section 19.

Because of the way in which new inventions are altering the pattern of demand, many people can expect to have to change jobs at least once during their working life. In order to make this easier, governments have introduced redundancy payments and unemployment benefit which, for a time at least, is related to the earnings in the last job. Advice is available through Job Centres, and there are government retraining schemes for those who need to learn new trades.

1 How do firms try to resist a falling demand? (Refer to Section 14.)

b) The supply may not be equal to a rising demand.

We might expect that the immediate response to this situation would be a rise in price, but we saw in Section 17.1 that where the market is dominated by a few large firms this is usually not so. One immediate response might be less advertising, which is of course equivalent to an increase in profits just as much as is raising the price. Other responses with consumer durables such as cars might be longer delivery dates and poorer service.

What happens in the long term depends on many factors. In some cases, increased output enables firms to cut the cost per article and therefore make larger profits without raising the price, e.g. the oil industry with larger tankers and larger refineries. The larger profits are used to repay bank loans which were raised to finance the expansion, and to provide funds for further expansion. (In recent years, finance for the expansion of industry came from retained profits 46%, bank loans 32%, government grants etc. 20%, the Stock Exchange 2%.)

In other cases, prices may rise steeply, and this is particularly true of raw materials. For example, if the demand for copper exceeds the supply, the price on the world market will rise rapidly. This has two effects: it encourages consumers to try to find cheaper substitutes, thus decreasing demand, and it makes the mining of low-grade ores a more profitable proposition, thus increasing the supply. Thus the price mechanism helps to ensure the efficient allocation of resources and adjust supply to demand.

2 Why might firms respond to increased demand by spending less on advertising rather than by increasing the price?

3 Explain as fully as you can who decides how the market will respond to changes in demand. (Refer to Sections 10 and 16.)

4 What would you expect to be the short-term and long-term effects of a rise in the demand for beef?

5 a) What would you expect to be the effect of a rise in the price of oil relative to the price of coal, gas, and electricity?
   b) A government might try to keep down the cost of oil to the consumer by a subsidy, i.e. by paying part of the cost of production directly to the producer, from taxes. What would be the effect of a subsidy on oil?

6 Which of the following decisions are made on the basis of choices by individuals as indicated by how they spend their money:
   a) That more sweets or more cigarettes will be produced?
   b) To produce a car with shock absorbers which last 30 000 miles or produce a car with shock absorbers which last 100 000 miles?
   c) To produce more beer and cigarettes, or more roads?
   d) Which postal service to use?
   e) To have more hospital places or more university places?

17.5 How efficiently is demand being satisfied?

We have now seen how the prices/profits mechanism is supposed to act as a means of allocating resources in order to ensure that the consumers' demands are satisfied as efficiently as possible. If a firm is satisfying a demand efficiently it should be able to make a high profit which can be used to expand to produce more of the products which consumers have shown that they want by being prepared to pay a high price for them.

However there are a number of ways in which this mechanism may not operate smoothly. Firms may try to obtain an artificially high price (see 17.2) and they may use their profits not for expansion but for dividends for shareholders and higher wages for workers. It is therefore not satisfactory to use 'profit' as a means of comparing the efficiency of firms.

For most purposes it is more realistic to compare firms (and countries) by analysing the 'added value'. Added value is the difference between the value of the goods (or services) produced and the costs of materials (and bought-in services) used in making them. That is, it is the wealth created by the enterprise.

Table 17C compares the added value and the way in which it is used for a selection of companies in Britain and a roughly comparable selection of companies in Japan (one of our main industrial competitors). Table 17D makes a similar comparison for British Leyland and Toyota of Japan. The negative tax for British Leyland is because it was in fact 'borrowing' money from the government.

1   What conclusions can you draw about the relative efficiencies of British and Japanese industries, and in particular the car industries?

2   What might the government do to try to improve the performance of British industry?

17.6 Workers cooperatives

We have seen that in Britain our present private enterprise economy is very owner/manager orientated. It is the owner/manager who takes the initiative in raising the capital from shareholders and employing workers to produce the goods. The managers feel responsible to the shareholders rather than to the workers. The result is that many workers feel their interests are in conflict with those of the managers and the shareholders. They therefore use their union strength to obtain an increasing percentage of the added value, perhaps to the detriment of the survival of the firm, as we saw in Section 17.5.

In the Basque region of Spain at Mondragon there has for some time been a successful example of a different form of organisation, a workers cooperative. Read Document 17B. More recently in Britain workers have taken over firms which were going bankrupt or have started cooperatives after being made redundant.

1   Can you give any examples of workers cooperatives in Britain?

2   One cooperative in Britain started by having a flat-rate wage for all workers. What difficulties do you think would arise in the long term from this policy?

3   What do you think the decision-making procedure should be for deciding questions such as wages policy?

4   If the majority of firms were organised as workers cooperatives, what difficulties might arise for trade unions?

5   Do you think there would be any advantages to the economy as a whole if industry were organised mainly as workers cooperatives?

17.7 The alternative of a planned economy

We have seen that in our 'market' economy the way in which resources are allocated to produce what the consumer demands is achieved mainly through the prices and profits mechanism. However, we have become aware that this market economy experiences a number of problems. For example, most of us would like stable jobs, but as consumers we would like production to change according to our changing demands for different goods. How can we reconcile these?

Are there other ways in which resources could be allocated which might overcome some of these problems?

You may know that in Communist countries the raw materials, factories, and capital are all owned by the State, and the way in which resources are allocated to the production of various types of goods is decided by government planning.

1   What will the planners need to know in order to do their planning?

2   Suppose it is decided that 100 articles 'X' are required each week.

You are the manager who is told to set up a factory to do this. You must calculate your needs in the way of machinery and workers, and these will be provided. If you do not meet your target, you will be transferred to a much lower-paid job. You calculate that, provided there are no breakdowns or other disruptions, you would require either 2 type-A machines, 10 type-B machines and 100 workers, or 1 type-A machine, 15 type-B machines and 75 workers. What will you ask for to *ensure* that you meet your target?

3   Now suppose you are the owner/manager of the same factory under a market economy. The annual cost of type A is £1000, type B £10000, and a worker £1000. In what way will you organise your factory?

4   In what way might resources be 'wasted' in a planned economy which would not happen, or not be so likely to happen, in a market economy?

In what way do you consider resources to be 'wasted' in a market economy which would not happen, or not be so likely to happen, in a planned economy?

Table 17A   *Percentage of total sales of various commodities accounted for by the five leading firms in each trade*

Commodity	Percentage	Commodity	Percentage
Bread	70	Bedding	33
Bacon	31	Pottery	45
Sugar	99	Cutlery	45
Margarine	97	Pharmaceuticals	34
Soap and Detergents	78	Paint	47
Beer	56	Wallpaper	92
Tobacco goods	99	Watches and Clocks	82
Footwear	28	Radios	78
Hosiery and knitted goods	36	Domestic electrical goods	60
Leather goods	16	Motor Vehicles	70
Women's outer clothes	17	Agricultural Machinery	31
Furniture	12		

Table 17B

Consumers' expenditure at 1975 prices

£ million

	1970	1971	1972	1973	1974	1975	1976	1977	1978	1979	1980
Household expenditure on food:											
Total.	12 041	12 090	11 988	12 181	12 091	12 058	12 155	1 994	12 331	12 575	12 651
Bread and cereals.	1 658	1 607	1 581	1 613	1 577	1 569	1 583	1 579	1 578	1 590	1 597
Meat and bacon.	3 408	3 416	3 322	3 208	3 233	3 326	3 328	3 398	3 483	3 593	3 609
Fish	404	391	386	375	334	363	364	335	343	352	387
Oils and fats	507	493	475	493	492	504	496	491	503	493	504
Sugars, preserves and											
confectionery	1 295	1 315	1 359	1 420	1 386	1 241	1 295	1 298	1 332	1 297	1 273
Dairy products.	1 504	1 600	1 609	1 652	1 635	1 636	1 635	1 573	1 591	1 581	1 565
Fruit	728	754	710	727	706	682	724	665	691	725	763
Potatoes and vegetables	1 464	1 463	1 492	1 554	1 522	1 463	1 396	1 422	1 533	1 564	1 584
Beverages	674	659	670	704	784	827	873	804	841	935	956
Other manufactured food	422	398	393	435	422	448	461	429	436	445	413
Alcoholic drink:											
Total.	3 668	3 912	4 212	4 776	4 892	4 856	4 938	5 023	5 313	5 575	5 367
Beer.	2 265	2 372	2 447	2 589	2 590	2 680	2 738	2 728	2 803	2 834	2 721
Spirits	880	933	1 062	1 317	1 408	1 342	1 312	1 370	1 487	1 644	1 553
Wines, cider and perry	547	632	719	· 870	894	834	888	925	1 023	1 097	1 093
Tobacco	2 701	2 605	2 747	2 918	2 885	2 748	2 653	2 523	2 746	2 731	2 685
Housing:											
Total.	8 443	8 714	8 917	9 181	9 081	9 221	9 238	9 406	9 693	10 091	10 024
Rent, rates and water charges	6 731	6 879	7 034	7 190	7 266	7 376	7 518	7 674	7 823	7 959	8 088
Maintenance, repairs and											
improvements by occupiers.	1 692	1 827	1 874	1 991	1 815	1 845	1 720	1 732	1 870	2 132	1 936
Fuel and light:											
Total.	2 782	2 752	2 854	2 930	2 984	2 914	2 887	2 959	3 013	3 179	3 073
Coal and coke	658	557	475	450	472	398	353	359	328	332	279
Electricity.	1 387	1 425	1 517	1 571	1 575	1 529	1 497	1 514	1 527	1 583	1 557
Gas.	534	566	628	656	714	772	818	859	934	1 044	1 064
Other.	206	204	232	253	223	215	219	227	224	220	173
Clothing:											
Total.	4 635	4 715	4 964	5 183	5 109	5 166	5 194	5 232	5 716	6 100	6 247
Footwear	752	762	792	816	822	941	863	858	949	1 003	972
Other clothing	3 883	3 952	4 171	4 367	4 287	4 325	4 331	4 374	4 767	5 097	5 275
Durable goods:											
Total.	3 987	4 750	5 770	6 064	5 302	5 367	5 641	5 224	5 932	6 595	6 337
Motor cars and motor cycles,											
new and second-hand.	1 759	2 345	2 811	2 668	2 033	2 135	2 222	2 009	2 401	2 596	2 381
Furniture and floor coverings.	1 335	1 396	1 596	1 650	1 522	1 592	1 645	1 499	1 582	1 790	1 800
Radio, electrical and other											
durable goods.	954	1 085	1 425	1 746	1 747	1 650	1 774	1 716	1 939	2 209	2 156
Other household goods	1 646	1 705	1 813	1 845	1 797	1 710	1 699	1 705	1 906	1 891	1 855
Books, newspapers and magazines.	979	985	1 024	1 016	994	941	911	907	915	932	930
Chemists' goods.	793	836	909	1 030	1 052	1 001	986	960	1 013	1 063	1 071
Miscellaneous recreational goods.	1 263	1 317	1 501	1 718	1 829	1 831	1 808	1 819	1 887	1 992	2 088
Other miscellaneous goods.	662	682	834	990	1 071	1 034	1 045	1 118	1 196	1 178	1 118
Running costs of motor vehicles:											
Total.	3 427	3 585	3 834	4 077	4 003	4 017	4 181	4 238	4 360	4 378	4 430
Petrol and Oil.	1 886	1 952	2 176	2 349	2 277	2 232	2 370	2 392	2 455	2 481	2 541
Motor vehicle and driving licences. .	336	347	362	378	372	400	404	404	424	426	451
Other.	1 186	1 264	1 288	1 350	1 354	1 385	1 407	1 442	1 481	1 471	1 438
Travel:											
Total.	1 879	1 881	1 999	2 121	2 068	2 042	1 969	1 957	2 030	2 096	2 176
Rail.	475	464	454	471	470	454	424	436	457	473	463
Bus, coach and tram	863	827	828	840	830	802	761	733	693	684	655
Air	315	344	444	528	481	514	522	527	603	641	741
Other.	253	268	281	282	287	272	262	261	277	298	317
Communication services	712	718	807	899	932	927	935	976	1 062	1 160	1 200
Entertainment and recreational											
services.	834	871	946	1 068	1 187	1 263	1 368	1 437	1 513	1 562	1 543
Domestic services.	314	291	286	286	286	293	298	298	297	295	305
Catering (meals and accommodation) . . .	3 183	3 122	3 296	3 322	3 239	3 260	3 247	3 268	3 241	3 350	3 323
Wages, salaries, etc. paid by private											
non-profit-making bodies	977	969	971	944	896	916	931	962	975	999	991
Capital consumption of assets owned											
by private non-profit-making											
bodies	127	129	135	141	148	155	162	170	177	184	190
Insurance	802	852	906	1 004	927	872	848	865	1 005	993	970
Other services.	2 429	2 572	2 688	2 676	2 611	2 524	2 491	2 591	2 615	2 865	2 745
Income in kind not included elsewhere . .	79	82	88	84	94	101	104	109	115	116	114
less Expenditure by foreign tourists in											
the United Kingdom	−977	−989	−1 053	−1 172	−1 290	−1 453	−1 746	−1 999	−1 876	−1 812	−1 655
Consumers' expenditure in the											
United Kingdom	56 942	58 787	62 255	65 282	64 188	63 764	63 943	63 742	67 175	70 088	69 778
Consumers' expenditure abroad	867	936	1 017	1 050	925	985	872	841	1 047	1 321	1 676
Total.	57 814	57 724	63 270	66 332	65 113	64 749	64 815	64 583	68 222	71 409	71 454

Source: Central Statistical Office

Table 17C *Comparison of added value per employee for a selection of companies in Britain and Japan*

(information from the Proceedings of the Institution of Mechanical Engineers Vol. 190 16/76)

	Britain (£)	Japan (£)
Total assets per employee	9036	27994
Net tangible assets per employee (buildings, plant, machinery)	3163	7634
Performance per employee:		
Sales	10969	26743
Raw materials and services bought-in	7694	19357
Added value	3275	7386
Distribution of added value:		
Wages, salaries, welfare, pensions	2128 (58·9%)	3471 (47·0%)
Rent, interest on capital	144 (4·4%)	1263 (17·1%)
Taxes	446 (13·6%)	842 (11·4%)
Dividends	151 (4·7%)	265 (3·6%)
Depreciation	303 (9·2%)	1101 (14·9%)
Retained profits	303 (9·2%)	444 (6·0%)

Table 17D *Added value per employee for British Leyland and for Toyota*

(Same source as Table 17C)

	British Leyland (£)	Toyota (£)
Total assets per employee	1924	22916
Net tangible assets per employee	1730	8127
Performance per employee:		
Sales	7664	42406
Raw materials and bought-in services	4835	34798
Added value	2829	7608
Distribution of added value:		
Wages, salaries, welfare, pensions	2592 (91·6%)	3545 (46·6%)
Rent, interest on capital	82 (2·9%)	122 (1·6%)
Taxes	−13 (−0·4%)	989 (13·0%)
Depreciation	200 (7·1%)	2320 (30·5%)
Retained profits and dividends	−32 (−1·2%)	632 (8·3%)

Document 17A   *How du Pont's Corfam took $100m caning*

(From *The Sunday Times*)

When the American chemical giant Du Pont announced on Wednesday that it was dropping its synthetic leather material, Corfam, it did more than write off 18 years' research and $100 million development.

It also destroyed a myth – the myth that the world's most sophisticated chemical company, whose scientific and marketing skills had built it up to £1500 million a year of world-wide sales, could somehow guarantee that these skills would turn a scientific breakthrough into a commercial profit-earner.

What went wrong? In global terms the idea looked a winner. Du Pont made a confident forecast in 1959, four years after its 'new venture' team had begun work, that the world was going to run short of real leather and would urgently need a substitute. The human population was outstripping the number of hide-bearing cattle, and increasing affluence would mean that millions more would be buying shoes.

The market seemed readymade and in a way so was Corfam, for Du Pont had done research in the 1930's which showed that it was possible to make a permeable plastic sheet with leather-like properties. By 1953 two versions were at pilot-plant stage with a better technique using synthetic fibres, and by 1955 a 'semi-works' factory was in production. Up to that point nobody had done a proper market forecast. Du Pont was in the grip of what researchers call 'technology-pull'.

Four years later the company was ready to build the large-scale plant at Old Hickory, Tennessee. The first material to roll off was suede finish, because to make this needed one process stage less than the calf or patent-leather finish. But production costs proved too high and the suede market was swamped overnight when Hush Puppies, made from cheap surplus pig hides, hit the shoe market. That was blow number one.

Undaunted, Du Pont switched to the 'smooth' leather market. Unfortunately when it test-marketed 20000 trial pairs of shoes the material was just not permeable enough for heavy everyday use. The marketing men were terrified of winning a reputation for uncomfortable shoes, so they concentrated on the top end of the market.

Women buy three times as many shoes as men and most of them are for dressy wear. Permeability did not seem to matter so much in fashion shoes, and the profit margin looked better.

Again the marketing effort was tremendous. Sales rose fast initially despite the total lack of interest shown by the shop girls who actually sold the shoes. By 1968 Corfam sales had reached 40 million pairs of shoes a year. And there they stuck.

Once again the market was pulled from under Du Pont's feet. By 1968 what women wanted were PVC-type materials. To the chemist PVC looked the worst possible material for shoemaking. Surely it would create nothing but sweaty feet.

But once the fashion had switched to open heels, toes, and sides – the sandal pattern – the chemistry no longer mattered. PVC shoes were cheap and could be thrown away after a month. Corfam was more durable than leather. But who cared?

Should Du Pont have seen the pattern sooner and saved some of its lost millions? It is easy with hindsight to say yes. Du Pont's marketing preparations were as elaborate as they could have been. Not only had it looked at the world demand, it had commissioned university psychologists to make a 'comfort' study, because Corfam has different qualities from leather.

But the product had run away with the company. And there was one other blow to come, sometimes called the 'sailing ship' effect. The old leather industry invaded by Corfam began to improve its product so that it should have all the advantages of leather and those of Corfam as well.

The best sailing ships were made after the coming of the steamer. If Corfam did nothing else it pushed the tanners into the late 20th century.

Document 17B   *Basques show way for coop ventures*
(From *The Sunday Times*, January 1981)

Trade Unionists believe that an enterprise which started 25 years ago in a remote valley in Spain's Basque country as a tiny, experimental workers cooperative could provide a radical solution to the problem of fast-rising unemployment in Britain's most depressed areas.

Later this month a high-powered delegation from the TUC in Wales will travel to Spain, with representatives of the unemployed, to inspect what has become one of the most famous and most successful workers cooperatives in Western Europe. A similar visit is being planned by Sheffield City Council.

In contrast to the patchy record of British experiments, ranging from Robert Owen's New Lanark in the nineteenth century to the Scottish Daily News which collapsed in 1975, the 75 separate cooperatives, clustered around the little Basque town of Mondragon, 30 miles from Bilbao, have had a remarkable history.

There has only been one strike in the last quarter of a century and although unemployment in the Basque country is now running at more than 20% – nearly twice the Spanish national average – Mondragon has so far weathered the storm without a single lay-off. This has been achieved largely by moving the labour force around the various enterprises.

The group has not escaped unscathed, however. Margins have been slashed, and Mondragon is soon likely to turn in its first-ever overall loss.

Founded in 1956 by Father Jose Maria Arizmendi, a Basque priest who was a victim of Franco's oppression, Mondragon now has an impact reaching far beyond the mountainous confines of the Basque country. It employs 17 000 people, and has a combined turnover of nearly £250m.

The first, and now largest, cooperative, Ulgor, with more than 3000 employees, is one of Spain's leading producers of washing-machines and refrigerators, and there is a powerful and efficient machine tool sector.

Mondragon also controls one of the Basque country's leading savings banks – an integral part of the whole concept – and is heavily involved in technical training and education, running its own Basque language schools.

Over the past years, Mondragon has been growing at the rate of four or five cooperatives a year – an expansion financed both by the workers and the community. Roughly 20% of each cooperative's start-up capital has come from the workers, who pay an 'entry fee' of around £2000 a head, a further 20% is provided by the state from a special cooperative loan fund, and the final 60% is put up by Mondragon's own savings bank, the Caja Laboral, which with 64 branches attracts savings from traditionally thrifty Basques throughout the region. The bank currently has around £100m in deposits, plus substantial reserves. The bank is the nerve centre of the Mondragon experiment and many independent experts see it as the key to Mondragon's success. Not only is the Caja Laboral the main source of finance, it also plays a vital role in the setting up of new cooperatives and the day-to-day running of existing ones.

The bank is responsible for the launch of all new cooperatives, and preparations are highly planned. Only when the bank's new enterprise division is satisfied is a new cooperative given the go-ahead.

In theory, it is the workers themselves who have the hire-and-fire powers over the coop's top management. But, in practice, it is the Caja Laboral which monitors management performance and has the final word. Over the past year the bank has sacked more than a dozen chief executives.

Mondragon, is no workers' paradise. It demands – and gets – a high degree of personal and financial commitment from its employees. Trade unions, only recently legalised in Spain, are not encouraged, and play no part in the Mondragon set-up. Nor is it easy for a worker to recover his initial investment if he wishes to leave the cooperatives before retirement age. But those who stay benefit from a generous profit-sharing scheme funded from ploughed-back profits.

Basque nationalism, and economic self-interest, have jointly ensured grass-roots support for Mondragon. An independent survey by Dr Keith Bradley, of the London School of Economics, suggests that the Mondragon firms are better managed and more efficient than their capitalist counterparts elsewhere in Spain.

But the next four or five years will be testing ones. Just as the workers share in the profits, so they bear the cost of any losses. So far the damage has been minimal, but as the recession deepens in the Basque country it will pose new problems for Mondragon.

18 The private sector and the public sector

So far we have been looking at those goods and services which are produced by private individuals or companies and usually offered for sale in shops. We can choose whether or not we want to buy these goods and, if we choose to buy, we can usually choose between different makes. This is called the 'private-enterprise sector' of the economy.

But there are also two other ways in which goods and services are supplied. One way is through public corporations e.g. the gas boards, the Post Office, and the British Broadcasting Corporation. We can choose whether or not to send a letter, but if we decide to send a letter we must use the Post Office. In most cases where there is a public corporation, we can choose whether or not we buy, but, if we decide to buy, we have no choice of supplier.

The other way is through central or local government, e.g. medical services through the central government, or refuse-collection through local government. In these cases we have the service whether we want it or not, and pay for it through taxes or rates.

Public corporations, central government, and local government are called the 'public sector' of the economy.

In some cases, goods or services are provided partly through the private sector and partly through the public sector, e.g. there are houses which are built and sold by private companies and there are also houses which are built and rented out through local government.

1   Using a local rate-demand form, a recent copy of *Britain: an Official Handbook*, and any other sources of information you may choose, find out how the following goods and services are provided:
      Milk
      Water
      Sewage disposal
      Protection of property (from thieves)
      Electricity
      Roads
      Insurance
      Newspapers
      Television programmes

2   Because some public corporations have a monopoly, e.g. the Post Office, it might be thought that they could charge as much as they wished for their goods or services. How are the charges made by public corporations decided? (See *Britain: an Official Handbook*.)

3   Are there any instances in which you think it would be to the consumer's benefit to allow private enterprise to compete with public corporations?

4   Of the services which are provided for all by local or national government, which could not be provided in any other way, and which would it be possible to provide by private enterprise if it were so desired?

5   At present most insurance, including car insurance, is provided by private enterprise. What are the arguments for and against providing it through a public corporation?

6   How is the money raised to pay for the services provided by local government? How is it decided how much money shall be raised and how it shall be allocated to the various services?

7   What are the arguments for and against including a loan service for 'classical' records as part of the public-library service without extra payment by the borrowers?

19 How governments have tried to manage the economy

Since the 1939–45 War, all British governments have tried to achieve the following aims:

a)   economic growth at a faster rate,
b)   full employment, or at least a low rate of unemployment and a short duration of unemployment for those who become redundant,
c)   a low rate of inflation,
d)   a balance of foreign payments.

For many years the highest priority was given to keeping down unemployment, but more recently the highest priority has been the control of inflation.

In this section we shall explore each of these aims in some detail, and in the next section we shall look at some of the factors operating in the world today which make it increasingly difficult for any British government to achieve these aims.

19.1 Economic growth

The usual measure of economic growth is the gross domestic product (GDP). This is the money value of all the goods and services produced within a nation during the year. The gross national product (GNP) is the GDP plus the net income from investments abroad. The GDP per head of population is some measure of the material well-being of a country. Table 19A shows how various activities contributed to the GDP for 1979. Table 19B shows how the national income per person has increased in various countries over recent years. The GDP for Britain has shown a steady increase until very recently (it trebled between 1965 and 1975) but it has not increased as fast as that of most of our industrial competitors.

Some possible reasons which might account for an increase in GDP are as follows:

a)   there are more people working
b)   people work longer and/or harder
c)   workers use more equipment and/or more efficient equipment.

1   Which of these do you think is the most important reason for the increase of GDP in Britain?

2   Can you suggest any reasons why other countries have done better than Britain? (Refer back to Section 17.5.)

TABLE 19A Gross Domestic Product 1979

	£ billion	%
Primary sector (raw materials)		
Agriculture, forestry and fishing	3·8	2·3
Mining and quarrying		
(including N. Sea gas and oil, £5·1bn)	7·8	4·7
Secondary sector (manufacturing)		
Manufacturing	45·6	27·6
Construction	10·2	6·2
Gas, electricity, water	4·8	2·9
Tertiary sector (services)		
Transport	9·5	5·8
Communication	4·3	2·6
Distribution	17·1	10·4
Insurance, banking, finance	7·1	4·3
Housing	9·8	5·9
Other services (holidays, catering, etc.)	22·3	13·5
Public sector		
Administration and defence	11·8	7·1
Health and Education	11·0	6·7

TABLE 19B National Income per person 1975

	National Income per person, £	Average % rate of growth p.a., 1965–1975
Australia	2599	3·4
France	2532	3·8
Germany, West	2712	2·6
Japan	1811	7·2
Sweden	3402	2·5
UK	1667	1·8
USA	2856	1·6

3   If the GDP per head of population shows a steady increase over the years, as it has over the last twenty years, what will people expect to happen to their wages and living standards?

19.2 Full employment

Fig. 19A shows how unemployment figures have varied over the years.

Until recently full employment (or as near as possible) has been the main aim of governments in Britain, so that whenever unemployment has risen they have taken steps to reduce it by stimulating the demand for more goods. One way of doing this has been to reduce income tax so that consumers have more money to spend and manufacturing firms will respond by employing more people to produce more goods.

1 In what other ways can governments try to stimulate demand?

2 There may be a lag between the time when the government reduces income tax and the time when British firms are able to increase production to put more goods on the market. What is likely to happen during this time, and what will be its long-term effects?

3 How might firms increase the quantity of goods produced without taking on more workers?

4 In Fig. 19A it can be seen that as well as the cyclical (up and down) effect, there is an underlying tendency for the unemployment to rise. Can you suggest any reasons for this?

Even in times of relatively full employment, there will be unemployment caused by the decline of some industries and the establishment of new industries – refer back to 'Labour with appropriate skills' in Section 10.1.

Figure 19A. Unemployment and vacancies

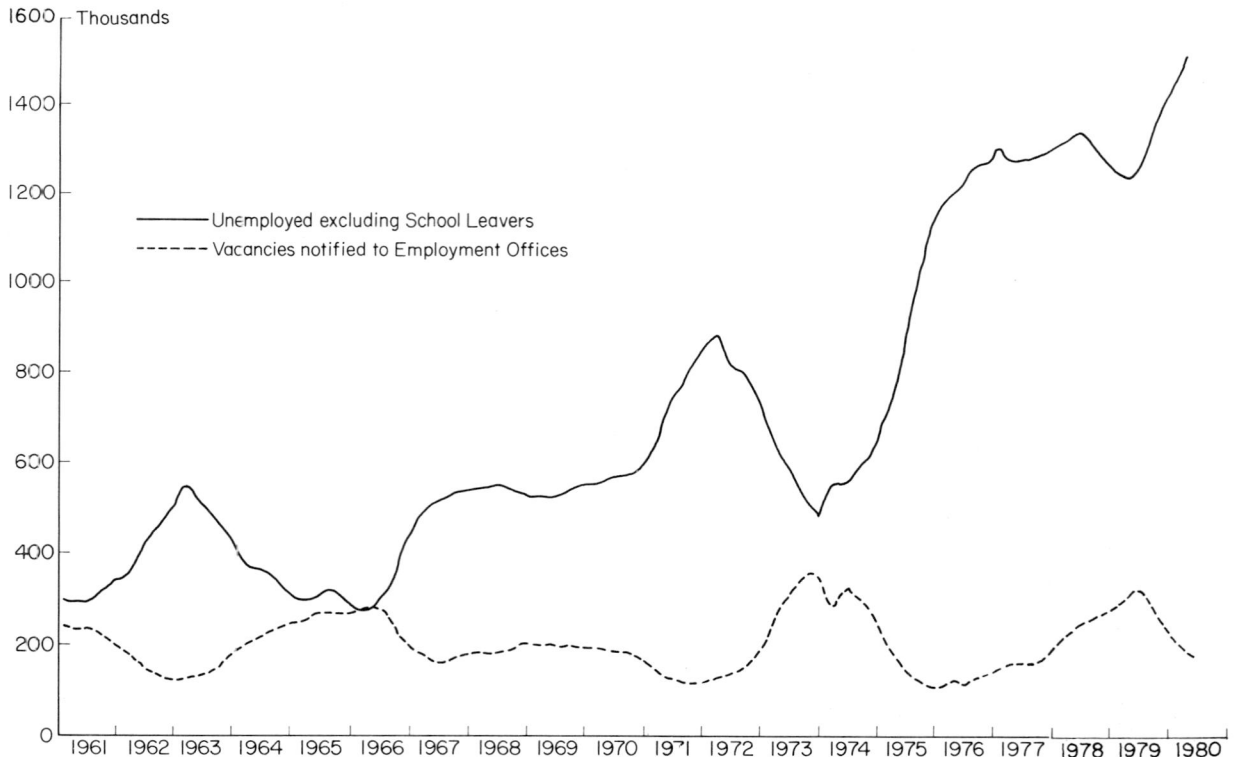

5 The new industries are likely to be established in parts of the country away from the declining industries. Why is this?

6 Not only are the new industries likely to be in different places, but they may require new skills. What problems are caused by these two factors?

7 What have governments done to try to alleviate these problems?

19.3 Control of inflation

A sudden sustained rise in prices is called inflation. One way of measuring price changes is by the retail price index (RPI). Market research techniques (see Section 2) are used to find out what goods and services are bought by a 'typical' household and at what prices. The total for the period chosen as a starting point is scaled up to 100, and the totals for other periods are scaled up correspondingly. For example, suppose we choose as a starting point the period January 1970 and the expenditure for a typical household for that period was £50 per week. The total for December 1972 is, £61. Then if the index for January 1970 is taken as 100, the index for December 1972 is 122.

Fig. 19B plots the average index for each year since 1972.

1 In terms of what money will buy, what was the approximate percentage increase in real wages between December 1972 and December 1975?

2 What are the bad effects of inflation?

3 Which sections of the community will suffer most?

4 In what way are some pensions and savings protected against inflation?

There are a variety of possible causes of inflation – the difficulty is to know which causes are the most important at any one time.

a) Suppose the average household feels able to spend up to £20 a week on food, and the cost of the average family bill is £18. The shopkeepers would be able to push up their prices to £20 before people would start buying less. This sometimes is called 'too much money chasing too few goods', or 'damand-pull' inflation. It can happen in general when the purchasing power of consumers or the money supply rises ahead of the output of producers.

b) Producers' costs might rise. There might be an increase in the price of imported raw materials, or powerful trade unions might obtain wage increases which are not accompanied by more goods being produced, or a fall in demand might result in a higher cost per article (see Section 3). This is often called 'cost-push' inflation.

5 How might the measures which a government takes to cure unemployment cause inflation?

Figure 19B. Inflation

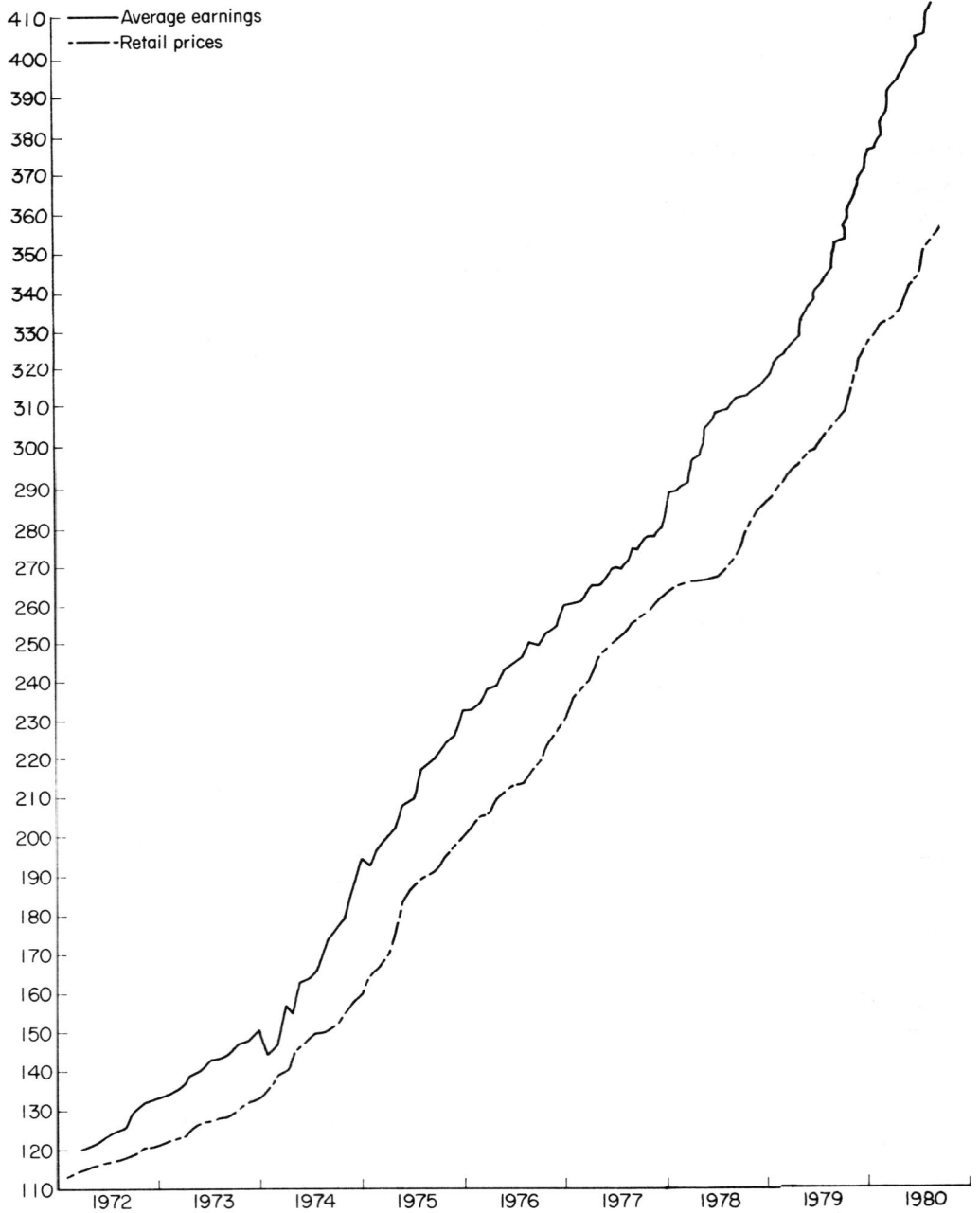

6 Why did the Thatcher government give a high priority to controlling inflation, and what means did it use?

7 Why might the means used to control inflation tend to cause an increase in unemployment?

19.4 The balance of payments

Table 19C gives a simplified picture of Britain's overseas trade for 1979.

For each of the items except 'invisibles' work out the difference between the value of exported goods and the value of imported goods. What is the total difference? This difference is called the balance of trade (or strictly 'the visible balance of trade').

As well as importing and exporting goods, Britain also pays for services provided by other countries and earns money by the services which it provides, e.g. shipping, civil aviation, insurance, tourism and interest and investments. These are often called 'invisible' items.

The balance of trade plus the balance of invisible items is called the balance of payments on current account. What was the balance of payments for 1979?

(In addition to the above, capital is coming from other countries into Britain for investment, and capital from Britain is being invested abroad. The net capital flow would have to be added to the balance of payments on current account to give the total balance of payments.)

1 Study Table 19C. For what items is Britain an overall importer?

TABLE 19C Overseas Trade 1979

	Imports	Exports	(£ billion)
Raw materials	4·0	1·2	
Fuels	5·8	4·3	
Food, beverages, tobacco	6·5	2·9	
Manufactured goods:			
Chemicals	3·4	4·9	
Machinery	7·4	9·8	
Transport equipment	5·3	5·0	
Other manufactures	31·4	33·1	
Invisibles	20·8	22·3	

2 How does Britain pay for these imports?

3 Are there any reasons why it will have become increasingly difficult for Britain to balance its trade with the rest of the world?

4 What effect will the use of North Sea oil have had on the balance of payments?

5 When governments have tried to control unemployment by stimulating demand, they have made more money available to the consumer, e.g. by decreasing income tax. If this money is available before British firms have responded by producing more goods, what is likely to be the effect on the balance of payments?

Inflation itself tends to cause a balance of payments deficit. A particular product, which is manufactured in both Britain and West Germany, costs £1 in Britain and 5 deutschmarks (DM) in Germany. At the exchange rate prevailing at a certain time, £1 could be exchanged for 5 DM. As a result of inflation in Britain, the product some time later sells for £2 in Britain but still only 5 DM in Germany. If the exchange rate remains the same, British exporters will not wish to sell in Germany because they can get £2 in Britain but only the equivalent of £1 in Germany. On the other hand, German exporters will step up their efforts to sell in Britain because they can get twice as much in Britain as in their own country. The effect of inflation is, therefore, to increase imports and decrease exports, thus causing a balance of payments deficit.

6   Can you suggest a possible cure for these difficulties? Are there any disadvantages to the cure you suggest?

The difficulties of achieving economic aims 20

In Section 19.2 we saw that in Britain since the war there has been an underlying tendency for unemployment to rise. Some of the reasons for this we shall look at below.

Because the main aim of most governments has been to achieve reasonably full employment, they have responded to a rise in unemployment by stimulating demand, e.g. by lowering income tax or making credit more readily available. The effect of this has been to cause inflation and balance of payments difficulties, until these have become so acute that the government has been forced to deflate demand again, thus producing the cyclical effect illustrated in Fig. 19A. On each succeeding cycle unemployment, inflation and balance of payments have each become worse.

There have been a number of other longer term effects. Keeping employment at a high level has caused shortages of some types of skilled workers. They have been retained in declining industries and not been available to newer industries which might have developed, often giving a start to Britain's main industrial competitors (West Germany, Japan, USA). At the same time, high wages have made declining industries uncompetitive relative to those industries in other countries, and thus accelerated their decline.

At the same points in the cycle, money was made available to consumers before British firms were able to respond by producing more goods. The effect of this was to draw in manufactured goods from abroad, thus establishing a pattern of supply which made it more difficult still for British firms to compete even in Britain, particularly if the exchange rate was unfavourable (Section 19.4).

Maintaining high employment by demand management has become increasingly difficult because of the side effects it produces. We must, therefore, look at the possible causes for the underlying trend for unemployment to increase to see whether these can be tackled more directly.

Technological changes in the means of production

Refer back to Section 13.4 Case 6
Advances in technology have made it possible for more and more goods to be produced by fewer and fewer people. As we saw in the case study referred to, a firm must make the technological changes in order to remain competitive with its rivals abroad, but the overall effect is more unemployment. Ideally, the workers shed in this way should be available to produce more goods in other industries.

1   What technological changes have decreased the number of people

employed in some industry with which you are familiar? (e.g. farming)

2 What technological inventions just coming into widespread use are likely to cause a further sharp decrease in the number of people employed in many industries?

Cost of raw materials

In the recent past there have been some very big increases in the cost of raw materials imported from abroad, particularly oil. The effect of this has been to take money out of the British economy so that less is available for spending on other goods, and therefore fewer people are employed producing those goods.

3 What are the main oil producing countries?

4 How could some of the money taken out of the British economy by these countries be brought back?

Competition from newly developing countries

Newly industrialising countries such as South Korea are able to produce more cheaply some of the goods traditionally produced in countries such as Britain. This is partly because they have newer factories and partly

Developing
industry
in Korea

because the workers are less well paid. If other countries buy from them rather than from Britain, there will be fewer jobs in Britain.

5 Go into a hardware store and discover the country of origin of as many of the goods as you can. Name the newly industrialising countries.

6 What ways have been suggested of responding to this competition?

Population changes

About fifteen to twenty years ago the number of children born in Britain was high, and since then the birth rate has gone down very sharply.

7 Explain two ways in which these population changes will have made the unemployment situation worse.

21 Personal incomes and wealth

21.1 The distribution of personal incomes

'Everyone should receive the same income whether they work or not.' Would this work out in practice?

'Everyone who works should receive the same income whatever job they do.' Would this work out in practice?

Study Document 21A. What do you think decides how much people earn?

One boy decides to train as a civil engineer. Another, equally able, decides to train as an accountant. The training periods are very similar and, at the time when they start to train, civil engineers and accountants receive much the same salaries. Later in life the civil engineer, although good at his job, discovers that he can now earn very much less than his friend who became the accountant. What could have happened to bring this about? What actions do trades and professions take to try to prevent this kind of change occurring?

Refer back to Section 17.6, Question 2. What factors do you think should decide a system of wage differentials in a workers' cooperative if there were to be one?

21.2 The redistribution of personal incomes

If for any reason it is thought that the distribution of income among the population which results from the operation of the market economy is in any way 'unfair', then the taxes which are used to finance government expenditure of various kinds can be levied in such a way that they bring about a redistribution of income.

The important features of the system of taxation and benefits are as follows:

Taxes

Income tax. Each person earning above a certain amount pays this tax directly from his income, hence it is called a 'direct' tax. In most cases, the employer stops it out of the wages and pays it directly to a government department. Each person is allowed to earn up to a certain amount free of tax, the amount depending on personal circumstances (single person, married person, mortgage interest payments, etc.). Above that figure, tax is paid at various rates which increase with income, so that, in general, the higher the wages the higher the *proportion* (not just the amount) paid as income tax.

National Insurance contributions. These are weekly payments by both employees and employers which go to finance National Insurance benefits (see below). As with income tax, the employee's contribution is stopped out of his wages and paid directly to a government department. The National Insurance contribution is dependent on the amount the worker earns.

Customs and Excise duties which are paid as part of the purchase price of a limited range of goods – mainly tobacco, alcoholic drinks, and petrol. These are examples of an 'indirect' tax.

Value Added Tax (VAT). VAT is a tax paid as part of the shop price of most goods and services except food. It was originally 10% of the final purchase price, but it can be varied according to circumstances (see Section 19), and at the time of writing it is 15%. Again, this is an 'indirect' tax.

Benefits

Family Income Supplement is an amount paid *to* workers with low wages according to their family circumstances.

Child benefits are paid to the *mother* according to the number of children.

National Insurance benefits – sickness benefit, unemployment benefit, old-age pensions, etc.

1   In some methods of taxation, people pay a higher proportion of their income as their income increases – not just more, but a higher proportion. These are called progressive taxes. In other methods, people pay a lower proportion of their income as their income increases. These are called regressive taxes.

   Which of the present direct taxes do you consider to be progressive and which regressive?

2   Do you consider an indirect tax such as VAT to be progressive or regressive?

3   If government expenditure increases, financed by higher taxation, does this necessarily benefit less-well-paid workers at the expense of higher-paid people?

4   Many of the benefits can be considered as 'transfer payments', transferring income from one section of the community to another. For example, family allowances transfer income from those who do not have children (through taxation) to those who do. What transfers are represented by sickness benefit, unemployment benefit, old-age pensions?

5   Suppose the Common Market countries agreed to amalgamate National Insurance benefits. Who might gain and who might lose? Would you agree to the idea?

6   People on low incomes are sometimes said to be in 'the poverty trap'. For example, if a husband whose wage is so low that he is receiving the Family Income Supplement gets a wage increase or slightly better job, then the amount of the increase is stopped from the Supplement, so he is no better off.

Can you devise a system of income tax and benefits which would remove this 'poverty trap'?

Is it desirable to do so?

7 Compared with other countries, Britain has high direct tax but low indirect tax. Do you think this encourages economic growth?

21.3 The distribution of personal wealth

As well as income from employment, some people have income from wealth which is invested in various ways, such as shares in limited companies. Table 21A shows the distribution of personal incomes and wealth.

1 Can you explain why the distribution of wealth is more uneven than the distribution of incomes?

2 Do you think it is 'fair' that some people should inherit wealth? (Think of yourself as a father who has worked very hard to work up a business which he wishes to pass on to his children. Think of yourself as someone who does not have a rich father! Consider whether the keeping-together of inherited wealth benefits the community as a whole.)

3 In what ways do governments attempt to redistribute accumulated wealth?

TABLE 21A   The distribution of personal income and wealth

Tenth fractions of the population	Approximate % share of income	Approximate % share of wealth
Top 10%	30	75
Second tenth	12	15·6
Third	11	5·7
Fourth	11	2·4
Fifth	10	1·0
Sixth	8	0·3
Seventh	6	0
Eighth	5	0
Ninth	4	0
Tenth	3	0

Document 21A   *Case studies of personal incomes*

(Weekly earnings before tax, 1981)

Long distance lorry driver, 48, £150

Drives to Ireland and the Continent. Most trips last four days. Works on average 50 hours per week, which including overtime brings in £120 to £150 per week. He gets expenses for overnight stops, on which he makes a small profit.

Chief Accountant, 43, £240

Medium-sized London based company, controls an office staff of 20. Responsible to financial director. £12 500 per annum + use of a company car.

Financial Director, 43, £580

Large public company with a turnover of about £40m. per annum. Salary £25 000 p.a. with extensive fringe benefits such as car, free life assurance, generous non-contributory pension scheme.

Secretary, 26, £90

Personal secretary to the financial director, London office. £4500 basic salary with occasional overtime, plus Luncheon Vouchers. 4 weeks holiday per year.

University Lecturer, 48, £250

Lecturer in mechanical engineering, at top of salary scale. Long holidays. Occasional articles in magazines etc. bring in another £200 p.a.

Headmaster, 45, £280

Head of a comprehensive school with 1100 pupils.

Floorsweeper, 50, £80

Floorsweeper in a medium-sized Midlands engineering firm. Recently there has been little overtime and earnings have often been reduced by short-time working due to lack of orders.

Farm dairyman, 40, £108

Responsible for a herd of a hundred milking cows. Basic wage of £88 brought up to £108 by overtime. Free 'tied cottage', but must pay rates, fuel, etc.

A counter assistant in a store

A Bingo caller at a social club

Coal-face mine worker, 34, £155

Basic £103. Payments for overtime, shifts and 'payment by results' brought this up to an average £155. Some mines provide free or reduced price coal. Surface workers get less, average £127.

London bus driver, 34, £128

Driver of a one-man bus for London Transport. Basic £92. Various additional payments including overtime brought this up to an average £128.

Hairdresser, 28, £84

Assistant in a city-centre salon in the Midlands. Tips cause earnings to vary considerably.

Sales representative, 32, £145

Sales representative for a firm manufacturing domestic appliances. Basic wage of £100 brought up to £145 by commissions. Has use of a company car and draws expenses at a reasonably generous level.

(Salaries of sales representatives vary widely:

the above represents an average. The highest paid computer hardware representative earned over £57000 p.a.)

Sales assistant, 20, £70

Sales assistant in a clothing store. 15% reduction on goods sold by the firm is an additional benefit.

Toolmaker, 34, £122

Tool and jig maker in motor vehicle firm. Shift work, days and nights fortnight about. Recently lay offs due to recession have brought down average yearly earnings.

South London bingo caller, 38, £100

Works afternoons and evenings, with Sundays off.

Chairman of British Rail, 57, £1154

Sir Peter Parker was not the highest paid of the chairmen of State industries. Mr Robb Wilmot at ICL was on £150000 p.a. and Sir Michael Edwardes at BL on £100000. Mr Ian MacGregor has a complicated deal which could be worth over £1m. over three years.

Social consequences of business activities 22

From the end of the Second World War in 1945 until the late nineteen seventies was a period of great industrial expansion. During the latter part of this period, many people began to be concerned about some of the unintentional but harmful long-term effects of business activities. Immediate concerns about recession and unemployment have forced these long-term fears into the background, but if there is a renewed industrial activity, then these fears will reassert themselves.

The long-term concerns were mainly of three kinds:

1 That industrial and domestic waste will contaminate the environment.

2 That natural resources, particularly energy resources, will run out.

3 That there will be an increasing wealth gap between developed and underdeveloped countries.

22.1 Waste disposal

Domestic waste

There are three ways in which waste leaves your house: (i) up the chimney (if you burn coal, coke, oil or gas); (ii) as sewage; (iii) as refuse in the dustbin.

1 Describe what happens to each of the three kinds of waste when they have left the house, and in particular what *permanent* effects they may have on the environment.

The Deepham Sewage Treatment works, with the Edmonton Refuse Incinerator Plant in the background

2 Why did these effects increase in Britain during the sixties and seventies?

3 What steps have been taken during recent years to try to diminish these effects?

Industrial waste

In 1967 in Japan, 111 cases of mercury poisoning occurred resulting in 41 deaths, as a consequence of eating fish or shellfish taken from Minirmata Bay. The bay had been contaminated by waste from a factory using mercuric oxide. Outbreaks occurred also in other places.

4 Can you find any other examples of substances which are used, or have been used until recently, which might cause similar damage?

5 What steps do you think could be taken to prevent firms contaminating the environment with industrial waste? Discuss in particular how the steps you suggest would be financed.

6 Why does the disposal of the radioactive waste from nuclear power stations present particular problems?

22.2 Conservation of resources

1 During the sixties and seventies the amount of goods used up by each person in Britain increased considerably. How can you explain this? (Look back to Section 14).

2 For what kinds of goods do you think production has increased most over the last ten years?

3 A metal called chromium is used in alloys which form part of many metal products. It is estimated that, at the present rate of consumption, known supplies of chromium will last only for about 30 years. As the supplies run out, which of the following do you think are likely to happen? (It could be all of them):
a) the price of chromium will go up;
b) because the price goes up, it will become economic to mine metal ores which contain very little chromium;
c) there will be research to find substances which could be used instead of chromium;
d) it will become economic to get back chromium from refuse – called 'recycling'.

4 Increased consumption is caused by increased consumption per person and by increased population. It is very difficult indeed to forecast population changes very far ahead, because this involves assumptions about the continuation of present trends – e.g. whether parents will continue to have the same number of children per family. Some recent population predictions are:

	1980	*1990*	*2000*	
Britain	59·3	63·2	68·2	(million)
World	4269	5068	5965	(million)

What do you think will be the effect of trying to find room for another 9 million people in Britain by the year 2000?

Which do you think causes the greatest increased use of resources, an extra 9 million people in Britain or an extra 9 million people in India?

The resources on which we are most dependent are the 'fossil fuels' – coal, natural gas, oil. North Sea oil production will begin to decline before 1990 and world oil production begin to decline before 2000. If our energy consumption even only remains the same, there will be an energy crisis soon after the year 2000.

5 What would be the effect on our everyday lives of this energy crisis?

6 Two alternatives to oil as a source of energy are to expand coal production by sinking new mines (e.g. in the Vale of Belvoir) or building nuclear power stations. Why are there objections to these. (Read Document 22A.)

7 What other sources of energy are being investigated?

22.3 The wealth gap between developed and underdeveloped countries

In your geography lessons you may have studied India. If so, you will have realised that life for most people in an economically underdeveloped country such as India is very different from life for most people in an economically well developed country such as Britain.

1 In what ways do conditions in Britain differ from conditions in India?

2 Make a list of countries which are similar to Britain, and another list of countries which are similar to India.

3 Look at Table 22A. India has a low income per person and a low rate of growth.
What are the reasons for this low rate of growth in income per person?

4 Find out what is meant by 'the Green Revolution'.

5 In developed countries, both birth rates and death rates are decreasing, but, because birth rates are still somewhat higher than death rates, there is a gradual increase in population. In underdeveloped countries the birth rates are decreasing very slowly. What, then, must be the cause of the rapid increase in population in underdeveloped countries?

TABLE 22A   National Income per person, 1975

	National income per person, £	Average % rate of growth p.a., 1965–1975
Argentina	835	2·6
Australia	2599	3·4
Brazil	430	5·4
France	2532	3·8
Germany, West	2712	2·6
India	62	1·1
Iran	630	11·9
Jamaica	570	4·5
Japan	1811	7·2
Sweden	3403	2·5
UK	1667	1·8
USA	2856	1·6

6 In an economically developed country such as Britain, each year some of the national income is invested in new factories and machinery which in turn increase the flow of manufactured goods. What is to prevent this happening in economically underdeveloped countries?

7 How could developed countries best help developing countries? Study Document 22B.

8 Referring back to Section 22.2, what might prevent the standard of living in underdeveloped countries ever catching up with that in developed countries?

Document 22A *Nuclear Britain going critical*

(John Huxley, reprinted from *The Sunday Times*, June 1981)

Inhabitants of the small Suffolk parish of Leiston-cum-Sizewell will hold a referendum later this year. They will vote on whether they want Britain's first pressurised water reactor (PWR) built on their coastline.

The outcome is unlikely to change the course of history, but both the government and the electricity supply chiefs are uneasily aware that after Leiston comes a more formidable hurdle. Construction of the PWR was originally scheduled to begin in early 1983. However the timetable has slipped so badly that the timing of the initial public inquiry is likely to catapult the government's nuclear policy into prominence as an election issue.

The political consequences are sufficiently unpredictable for ministers to tread with great caution over the coming months. Indeed, it has already been suggested that the political resolve to push through the project is weakening. Nothing could be further from the truth.

The foundations of the government's nuclear policy, built upon the ruins of previous good intentions (see below), were laid down as long ago as December, 1979. They have been a source of confusion – some of it, no doubt, deliberate – ever since.

At the time, energy secretary David Howell talked of the need to order at least one new nuclear power station a year in the decade from 1982, equivalent to a programme of about 15 000 MW over ten years. This, however, was not a commitment. It was, rather, 'a reasonable prospect against which the nuclear and power plant industries can plan'. The precise level of orders would depend upon demand for electricity and the performance of the nuclear industry.

Convinced of the need to maintain the flow of orders to a nuclear industry in the doldrums, Howell approved the start of work on two advanced gas-cooled reactors (AGRs). Simultaneously, he approved plans by the electricity supply industry to order a PWR 'subject to the necessary consents and safety clearances'. There was even brave talk of work beginning in 1982.

Setbacks

Since then, orders for the AGRs have been placed and work begun. A reference design for a Westinghouse-type PWR at Sizewell has been submitted to the nuclear inspectorate by the National Nuclear Corporation.

However, since the beginning of this year the government and the chosen instruments of its nuclear policy have suffered a number of setbacks which together have made more difficult the task of winning public acceptability.

The Commons Select Committee on Energy in its report on the nuclear power programme levelled many serious criticisms both of relationships with the nuclear industry and of the economic basis on which power station need was being calculated.

A few weeks later, in March, the Friends of the Earth, published its critique of the PWR. They, too, found fault with demand forecasts on which nuclear needs were based.

Far more efficient to insulate lofts than build PWRs, Friends of the Earth argued. Safer, too. The report rehearsed many of the familiar arguments over safety problems within the PWR.

The report of the Monopolies and Mergers Commission on the CEGB, published in May, further undermined the economic case for a power station programme anything like as large as one Howell had talked of in 1979. Demand forecasting had been seriously inaccurate, and led to premature ordering of new plant and increased costs, the commission said.

The embarrassment increased when in the same week as the commission reported, Denis Rooney, the man recruited after a long search to strengthen the National Nuclear Corporation, resigned the chairmanship after serving less than a quarter of his four-year term of office.

The government has always wanted the NNC – comprising the Atomic Energy Authority, GEC and British Nuclear Associates (itself a troublesome amalgam of seven engineering companies) – reorganised and strengthened so that it could take on total project management responsibility for the first PWR.

Morale within the NNC remains high but brittle. Further evidence that the nuclear industry is divided – not least by continuing wrangles over the merits of AGR versus PWR – does not instil confidence that its members can build power stations on time and to cost.

The NNC remains a problem in the eyes of ministers. They are still not satisfied that the corporation, which has capital of only £10m, can bear the risk of building stations costing upwards of £1bn. Either the equity must be increased or other forms of risk-sharing devised.

Each of these developments – the reports and the departure of Rooney – has provided ammunition for opponents of nuclear policy be their reasons economic, political, ideological or financial. The issues have also become confused. The public inquiry into Sizewell B, instead of examining proposals for one station on one site, is likely to draw into question the whole nuclear programme.

The government's commitment has emerged from this battering dented but still intact. The prevailing view, forcibly espoused by Mrs Thatcher, is that the strategic reasons for going further nuclear remain compelling.

Norman Lamont, energy under-secretary and the minister overseeing the nuclear programme, insists, 'After a quarter of a century of generating electricity safely from nuclear power in this country, we know that it can make a major contribution to our future energy supplies.'

By the end of this century about 30% of Britain's electricity generating capacity could be nuclear. Some of our major industrial competitors will have surpassed that figure before 1985.

The most galling example is France, which already boasts a proportion of nuclear and hydro-electric power five times greater than Britain.

In more general terms the government believes the 1980's should be used to develop energy sources which will reduce the long-term dependence upon fossil fuels.

In the next few weeks, therefore, the government is likely to attempt to regain the initiative in a series of moves aimed at answering recent critics and providing a firm lead for the nuclear industry.

Ministers are planning a robust response to the Select Committee report covering also many of the criticisms made elsewhere. A paper is already being circulated in draft form and the finished product should be available before the summer recess.

Apart from restating the government's broad objectives and its recognition that ordering must be carried out on a step-by-step basis, the paper will reject suggestions that the Canadian CANDU reactor can be considered as another option. This is regarded as an unnecessary complication.

Meanwhile, no attempt will be made to find a new chairman for the NNC. Instead, the government is likely to confirm within the next few weeks that Frank Gibb, a joint managing director of Taylor Woodrow, can continue to act as chairman. He took over this role on the departure of Rooney.

As a senior executive of one of the NNC's member companies, Gibb cannot be the strong, independent chairman originally envisaged for the corporation. His appointment is bound to upset other companies within the NNC who saw in Rooney's departure further evidence of power politics on the part of the pro-PWR faction, headed by GEC. However, the alternative – finding a new acceptable chairman – is too daunting if not actually impossible. None of this is likely to bring a new sense of purpose to the nuclear industry.

For that the government is pinning its hopes on another director of the NNC, Dr Walter Marshall, chairman of the Atomic Energy Authority, who at the same time will be appointed to take charge of planning the PWR at Sizewell, and its possible successors. Marshall, an amiable but forceful man with a solid background in PWR research is seen in government circles as fulfilling the job of 'moderator' or 'honest broker' within the nuclear industry, acting as a 'catalyst' during the increasingly complicated design stages of the project.

These are now crucial to the success of the PWR plans and are the subject of a thorough review this summer. The government, and the teams working in the PWR, are now caught in the squeeze exerted by safety standards on the one side and cost constraints on the other. The difficulties involved in achieving a satisfactory trade off has been made worse by the tight time schedule.

The reference design already submitted is based on a Westinghouse reactor. Additional British safety standards are, in effect, being planned round it, and the CEGB has said that the PWR will be built to AGR safety standards.

Thus, for example, the Sizewell design has four independent cooling systems, instead of the more usual two. It also has a double walled containment, involving some 5 metres of additional reinforced concrete shielding, to reduce still further operating risks.

Will this mean that the PWR becomes too big, too complicated and too costly? The nuclear industry has to show that it does not, and that it is possible to build a PWR in Britain cheaply, but without cutting any corners on safety.

Document 22B *The Brandt Report*
(Leader from *The Sunday Times*, February 1980)

The most important event this year was the release last week of a small paperback book of 300 pages. It surfaced only briefly in the headlines, rapidly submerged by Mark Thatcher and his mother, Arthur Scargill and his bully boys, Kevin Keegan and his manager, and tremors from Teheran to Lake Placid. That in itself is part of the problem. The book has more real meaning for all our lives than any of the clamour which routinely assails us. But to canvass it with headlines invites the level of attention enjoyed by the man with the sandwich board daily proclaiming that tomorrow is the end of the world. The warning in the paperback is more credible but it is more complex. What threatens mankind – and it is as large a peril as that – is a lethal and unpredictably volatile mixture of starvation, inflation, escalating unemployment, international monetary disorder, protectionism, major tension between countries competing for energy and food and raw material, growing world population, advancing deserts, over-fishing, pollution of air and water, and the arms race.

These are not doomsday hysterics from Los Angeles. The paperback *North–South, a Programme for Survival* is the report to the United Nations of the Brandt Commission, gathering up two years of independent study by 18 world leaders and Willy Brandt, the former German Chancellor. They did not expect to agree. They came with different experiences and convictions from many parts of the world. They argued a lot. But they reached a chilling consensus.

The world economy is breaking down. There are eighteen million people out of work in the West. More join them every day. A number of poor countries are threatened with the irreversible destruction of their ecological systems. Deforestation at present rates will halve the world's stock of wood by the year 2000 (with increased carbon dioxide pollution among other effects). World population grows by one million people every five days. There will be another two billion people to feed in the next two decades. There are already eight hundred million absolute poor, and the number grows.

The Brandt report is crammed with laconic detail which puts our own concerns in shameful perspective. In the poorest countries, one child in four dies before reaching the age of five. In 34 countries over 80% of the people are still illiterate. A little over £1 a child would immunise every new born baby in the Third World against the commonest diseases. We consume, per head, a hundred times as much energy as people in the poorest countries; one American uses as much oil as 1072 Nepalese. The best comment on all this is in an interview in Tatler with Miss Mandy Rice-Davies, re-emerging from the Sixties. 'I am very, very worried about the Western world,' she says, 'There are far too many people running around in Gucci shoes.'

We cannot count on altruism. Even during the biggest boom in human history, most rich countries have failed to reach their minimum targets for aid. The Brandt Commission is wise, therefore, to emphasise self-interest. We are all in this up to the neck. The world system is now so interlocked that no one can escape the consequences. Between 1973 and 1977 trade with the Third World created jobs for nearly 5 million people in the North. A third of all our exports go to the Third World. To buy them, Third World countries need support for their deficits, and fair prices and fair access for their trade. That shows how futile protectionism is: one of the sadder aspects of politics in Britain has been the way socialism, once an international movement, is now reduced to whimpering behind the barriers of a siege economy. There is no future in that. The North cannot expect to export more, creating more jobs and prosperity, unless it provides improved access to its own markets. As it is, the North exports nearly four times as much in manufactures to the South as it buys from it. Older industries in the North need time to run down, certainly; but it is crazy to keep out cheaper products from the South. They help consumers everywhere. They reduce inflation. Bridging the gap between rich and poor is not only humane: it opens up a potential market of 2000 million poor people. Nothing else will solve the North's problem of over-capacity, or ensure survival for the South.

A sense of futility is natural. But the technical answers are there. What is required is the political will. Brandt's commissioners spell out practical measures which the citizen can press on his politicians. The programme cannot be dismissed as cranky. What is more eccentric, one might wonder, than having a steelworks in Llanwern lie silent while India laments a steel shortage? No less than £170000 million worth of productive capacity lies idle in the North, while the South cries out for its products.

Brandt calls for a world summit this year, to consider an emergency programme with four key elements: a massive transfer of funds to developing countries: an international energy strategy: a global food programme: and a start on reform of an international monetary and financial system devised for a very different world. Priority must be given to the needs of the poorest: and most of the help for them will have to come from official aid. This is the year by which the rich countries had promised to reach aid levels of 0·7% of GNP. We are only half way there: the Brandt Commission calls for firm timetables to reach that figure by 1985 and provide another £13 billion a year.

For those middle-income countries for whom debt-servicing alone now accounts for at least 20 per cent of export earnings, there must be either increased loans financed by the World Bank or Government guarantees for commercial loans. At last – and it is a familiar theme to Sunday Times readers – there is a sensible proposal on oil. Brandt proposes a strategy in which oil exporters would guarantee supplies, the West would pledge itself to consume less extravagantly, and sudden price increases would be avoided. Prices could be indexed to world inflation and protected from currency fluctuations.

To bring order to the monetary system, Brandt insists that the role of the International Monetary Fund should be expanded. More credit could be created by Special Drawing Rights. Between now and 1985, Brandt estimates, up to £200 billion needs to be added to the debts of developing countries if growth is to be sustained. That will require not only guarantees but the creation of concessional funds to ease the cost of borrowing. To squeeze countries like Turkey to the point of anarchy is a sophisticated form of lunacy.

There is an even more radical set of proposals in Brandt which deserve support. Automatic transfers of resources would allow developing countries to plan their policies independently of the whim of donors. Brandt proposes a sort of international income tax, with levies calculated on a sliding scale related to national income. There could also be levies on international travel, or military expenditure and arms sales, or the mining of seabed minerals. It is an extraordinary fact that the cost of a modern fighter would pay for 40000 village pharmacies. Some automatic schemes like this may be the only way to protect ourselves against shortsighted politicians of the kind who, in a North–South meeting in Delhi last week, vetoed a proposal for an industrialisation fund.

In Britain, preoccupied with problems incapable of solution nationally, we are going up a blind alley with policies for reducing aid and for limiting retraining which run directly counter to Brandt's proposals. Instead of structural reform, the government is addicted to patching up the existing systems, murmuring about living in the real world. But it is Brandt and his colleagues who are living in the real world. Perhaps the young, tired of the rivalries, insularities and inertia they inherit, will embrace that better vision.

23 How decisions are made

23.1 The decisions to be made

In Parts 1 and 2 of this study we were concerned with setting up, and subsequently enlarging, a business enterprise which would make a profit. We could argue that in doing this we have contributed to the nation's prosperity, that we have been able to provide for the comfort and security of our families, and that we have also given opportunities to our employees to do likewise.

In Part 3, however, we have stood back and viewed our business activities from a wider perspective. In Section 17, for example, we saw how the prices/profit mechanism is the chief means by which resources are allocated in our type of economy. More generally, we have also seen that some of the decisions it seemed necessary and wise to make for the sake of our business could have profound implications for contemporary society, for future generations, and for people living in other parts of the world. With these considerations in mind, we may feel we should give additional weighting to social factors in our gains and losses accounts, because unless the creation of wealth leads to an improvement in the quality of life, it has little justification for its own sake.

Fortunately, we live in a democratic society, which means each of us can have some influence on the kind of society ours shall be, what values it upholds and the degree to which it cares for its weakest members. Here are ten questions that arise out of the activities with which you have been concerned on this course. People do not agree about the answer to these questions so they are worth debating in class. Sooner or later you will be expected to have your own point of view about them:

1   What should be a government's priorities in trying to manage the economy?

2   Which industries should be publicly owned?

3   Should there be limits on individual wealth?

4   Can the amounts that are paid to people who do different jobs be justified?

5   Should people accept less pay so more can be employed?

6   Should house owners and firms pay rates?

7   Should Britain withdraw from the EEC?

8   What should be done about the energy crisis?

9 Should Britain set an example of unilateral disarmament?

10 Should greater efforts be made to help the poorer nations in the world to become richer?

Most of us are prepared to accept some restrictions on our freedom of action for the benefit of others. What would it be like, for instance, to have no laws or no police force to ensure that the laws were kept? Most of us are prepared to make sacrifices for members of our own families or our friends, or at least to allow them to share to some extent the good fortune that we may have at any time. However, the big question that we all have to answer is how far we are prepared to extend our willingness to share our wealth and to restrict our self-interest. To family and friends, maybe, but what about including neighbours, or the poor and needy in different parts of the country or even the world, or generations yet unborn?

If you look again at the ten questions, you will see that the problems some of them raise could only be satisfactorily resolved by some kind of agreement among the wealthy industrialised nations of the world; others might be the subjects of debate in the European Parliament. Most of them, however, form the key issues that are put before the electorate by the four main political parties at the time of a General Election. Do you know which are the four main political parties in this country? How would politicians representing each of these parties be likely to answer each of the ten questions?

During the course of this study of our industrial society you will have come across examples of actions and practices which are perfectly legal, but for some reason you do not agree with them and you feel strongly that they should not be allowed. Political parties may express different points of view about some of them in their manifestos and then when you are eighteen these will help you decide for that candidate who comes nearest to representing your opinion. Many of the issues that you feel strongly about, however, may not figure in any party political manifesto. How then can you bring about a change or influence decisions that may be taken on these issues?

You must first understand the way in which decisions are made at top level in British government; secondly, you must know who the decision-makers are; and thirdly, you must be aware of the best methods of influencing the decision-makers.

23.2 The decision-makers

It is not our purpose here to give a long detailed account of the British system of government, but it is important to have a general idea about how things are done in Britain.

First, we must understand that Britain, unlike many other countries, has no single document legally and specifically defining the nature of its government and the relationships between the various institutions that make up the government. The British system of government has been fashioned by tradition over the centuries to meet the particular interests of the nation. On the one side it reflects the independence, stability, and unity that the country has enjoyed and, on the other, many of those characteristics that have become regarded as typically British, e.g. the desire for strong government yet a certain distrust of 'the expert', the loyal support given to one or the other of the two main political parties by the vast majority of the electorate, and the lack of noisy and ostentatious displays at election times.

At least every five years the country has the opportunity to choose a new government. Traditionally, the Queen will ask the parliamentary leader of that political party which has by election secured most seats in the House of Commons to form a government. Thus the new Prime Minister (who may be the old one if their party has been successful again) chooses the Cabinet ministers, who collectively accept the responsibility for the government of the country. The decisions this team takes and the measures it proposes have to be justified first in the House of Commons, then in the House of Lords, and finally receive the Queen's assent. As the government can count on the votes of its backbench party members, who form the majority of MP's in the House of Commons, its propositions are not likely to be defeated there, although amendments are often made in the light of adverse criticism. Nor can the House of Lords (since the Act of 1949) delay the passing of a Bill for longer than twelve months. The Queen's assent has become more or less a formality. Hence, as a general rule at least, the Cabinet is responsible for governing the country, and Parliament is simply the place where decisions have to be justified, but not often made.

It seems, then, that in Britain the Prime Minister and the Cabinet are given a relatively free hand to make and implement major decisions. There are of course some constraints, the greatest of which is the knowledge that to a certain extent their performance in office will be judged at the next general election. Similarly, most ministers are sensitive to criticism in Parliament and, although they can normally rely on the votes of their backbenchers in the House of Commons, they know that at their own political party conferences their actions may meet more outspoken condemnation. But the British people like their governments to have strong leadership, which is neither afraid to govern nor impeded from doing so. This is the prime reason why national referenda have never been popular in this country, nor noisy, violent public demonstrations very effective, but can you think of exceptions?

23.3 How the decision-makers are influenced

So we have identified our top decision-makers: the forty or so government ministers, especially those some twenty who are members of the Cabinet. However, two questions still need to be answered:

1   how do they arrive at their decisions?

2   do they in practice make all the decisions of government?

The volume of work of each ministerial department has grown so enormously in the twentieth century that ministers can no longer be acquainted with every important issue. Consequently, there are now over 400 000 officials in Whitehall whose job it is to advise ministers. By far the greater proportion of decisions that have to be made are routine and non-controversial, arising out of the ordinary business of administration. It has become established practice for these decisions to be made by senior civil servants, albeit in the name of the minister, who may be called upon to justify them in Parliament. On those questions that are likely to cause political controversy, a Permanent Secretary has to decide whether to put them before the minister, who, in turn, has to decide whether to take them to the Cabinet. Similarly, when ministers wish to introduce one of their own ideas, they will first discuss it with senior officials, and then put detailed proposals before their colleagues in the Cabinet for their criticisms and the criticisms they anticipate they will receive in Parliament. If the proposed measures stand up to this onslaught, they will eventually be implemented. If they do not, the minister may resign from the Cabinet, but this is a rare occasion.

It is clear, therefore, that the Civil Service plays a fundamental role in the processes of decision-making. But senior civil servants, like ministers, are not expert, in a technical sense, in many of the issues that are the direct concern of their departments. They, too, must spend much of their time listening. The spokesmen to whom they listen hold the key to the machinery of decision-making.

These spokesmen who have the ear of Whitehall are the representatives of interested groups: the various trade unions, the Farmers' Union, the Confederation of British Industry, the Howard League for Penal Reform, the RSPCA, the AA and the RAC, the Central Council for Physical Recreation and the Association of British Chambers of Commerce – to name but a few. Each department has its own collection of groups whom it traditionally consults about particular interests. This process of consultation is valued alike by the government and by the groups concerned. On the one hand it provides the government with information, and on the other it provides the groups with prestige in the eyes of their members.

23.4 Campaigning for change

Now, name one aspect of British industrial society which you would like to see changed. It must be more than just wishful thinking and some aspect that can either be implemented or changed through legislation. Make out a detailed plan of campaign which you would use to give your proposals the greatest chance of acceptance by the government, clearly indicating the four or five steps that it would be necessary to take.

Index

The authors and publishers would like to thank the following for permission to reproduce the photographs and other illustration material in this book (page numbers in brackets):

British Steel Corporation (6), *Farmers Weekly* (6), Joseph Lucas Ltd (6), Esso Petroleum Co. Ltd (6), *Punch* – Handelsman (17), Companies Registration Office (19), WCB – Clares Ltd (21, 25), Montague Burton Ltd (28), Spar (28), Comet (30,37), The Boots Co. Ltd (33), John Lewis (35), The Littlewoods Orgn Ltd (37), Fine Fare (36), Birkenhead and District Co-operative Society (29), Vending Centres (Holdings) Ltd (39), The Stock Exchange (56), Ford Motor Co. Ltd (63, 82), National Union of Railwaymen (72), Volvo Concessionaires Ltd (83), *Private Eye* – M. Heath (86, 109), Griffin and George Ltd (88), Sony (UK) Ltd (89), Autocar (89), Philips Electrical Ltd (90), Wallis and Co. (Costumers) Ltd (91), Kosset Carpets Ltd (94), Institute of Trading Standards Administration (104), British Standards Institution (105), British Electrotechnical Approvals Board for Household Equipment (105), *Punch* – M. Heath (107), Scientific and Technical (109), Ransom Hoffmann Polard Ltd (115), Hoover Ltd (116), Lever Bros Ltd (116), F. W. Woolworth and Co. Ltd (145), Mecca (146), BBC (147), Thames Water Authority (147), Bejam Freezer Food Centre Ltd (38), Keystone Press Agency (46), Andrew Wiard *Report* (72).

The authors and publishers are grateful to the following for permission to reprint copyright material:

The Sunday Times, Documents 14A, 17A, 17B (11.1.81) by Stephen Aris, 22A (28.6.81), 22B (17.2.80); Design, Document 14C; The Controller of Her Majesty's Stationery Office, Documents 11A, B, Tables 17A, B, 21A; Institution & Mechanical Engineers, Tables 17A, B.